To

WARRIOR POETS OF THE 21ST CENTURY

A Biblical and Personal Journey in Worship

Blessings to you

robin mark

warrior poets of the 21st century
A BIBLICAL AND PERSONAL JOURNEY IN WORSHIP

AMBASSADOR INTERNATIONAL
GREENVILLE, SOUTH CAROLINA • BELFAST, NORTHERN IRELAND

WARRIOR POETS OF THE 21ST CENTURY
A Biblical and Personal Journey in Worship

© Copyright 2007 Robin Mark

ISBN 978-1-932307-78-8

Published by the Ambassador Group
Cover — Mark Graham
Interior — David Siglin

Ambassador Publications
Providence House
Ardenlee Street
Belfast
BT6 8QJ
Northern Ireland
Email: ambassadorintl@aol.com
www.ambassador-productions.com

Ambassador International
Emerald House
427 Wade Hampton Blvd.
Greenville
SC 29609, USA
Email: info@emeraldhouse.com
www.emeraldhouse.com

Paul Reid, Senior Pastor of Christian Fellowship Church in Belfast, and my very good friend, says that "everybody has one sermon in them." In other words, everyone 'down there' in the congregation could probably manage to deliver one stirring sermon to the assembled faithful from 'up there' in the pulpit.

If Paul Reid says it, then it must be right. I'm hoping that the same is true for writing a book.

For some time now I have toyed with the idea of committing my jumbled thoughts on worship to the pages of a text that, with God's grace, might encourage some, challenge some, make some laugh, make others cry and, best of all, might be another act of worship on my part to the Father.

A recent proliferation in books on worship and a number of challenging articles in the Christian press haven't dampened my enthusiasm. If anything, I'm torn between a mixture of thoughts, such as: "Well, I may as well put in my tuppence worth, (two cents, if you're American)" and "Some of these folks just don't get it."

Like all writers, I suppose, I'm naively convinced at the outset that I have something new and dynamic to say and that this is a blockbuster waiting to bust all the blocks.

In truth, it's probably all been said before. And probably better.

I need to thank some people. Principally, my wife, Jacqueline, who read the first draft, and the second draft, and probably most of the four or five corrected drafts that followed those. This book would not be here without her help, love and assistance. Her thoughts, comments, directions and encouragement were, as always, totally invaluable.

Thanks also to the other folks who proofread various copies and gave valuable input. Particularly the very gifted Helen Mills, whose balanced encouragement, editing and correction was a real blessing at a critical stage. Also Paul Reid, Andrew Toogood, Katy Irwin, Ruth Morrison, Marilyn Toogood and Michelle Wooderson.

So here it is. It's not a workbook, it's not a theological tome, it's not a lifestyle modification book, it's not deep and it's not shallow. It's just a collection of thoughts that, with God's grace, will be a little of all of the above and, perhaps, a bit more to you.

Enjoy, and God bless.
Robin

CONTENTS

FOREWORD

I first heard Robin lead worship at a wedding in January 1987. He sang one of his early songs, O Behold the Lamb. It was one of those God-moments and in my heart I knew that this was the man who would partner me in building the fledgling Christian Fellowship Church in Belfast. He was soon to become our anointed psalmist who would lead us into God's presence. Week by week we discovered the treasures of praise and worship as the church grew in numbers and strength. Our friendship also grew and I learned to love this man as he led our church deeper into God. It's been twenty years and Robin continues to lead worship regularly in CFC to the present day!

What an adventure of faith, learning, laughter, tears and lots of fun! Little did we know where this journey would take us. Robin's songs became known and sung in churches of every denomination throughout Ireland and then internationally, particularly after the release of the CD, Revival in Belfast. The journey has taken him all around the world and there is rarely a Sunday that we don't have visitors from overseas who have come to hear him lead worship.

Worship is one of those subjects which, as we say in Belfast, 'is better felt than telt'. In this book, Robin puts down in print what he has learned and gleaned over the years. The opening chapters on what worship is, are, in my opinion, the best I have ever read on the subject. They are clear, precise and profound. Every church should hear this wisdom; it would dramatically enhance their understanding and practice of what has been called 'the believers highest occupation'.

But there is so much more contained within these pages. Robin reveals his experiences with humour, his understanding with clarity and, above all, his heart – his heart for worship, the Church, and the glory of God. This is the best book on worship I have ever read.

Read it yourself, buy a copy for every member of your church, and experience afresh the wonder of worship. Your church will never be the same again.

Paul Reid
Senior Pastor
Christian Fellowship Church
Belfast

June 2007

CHAPTER 1
Those Whom God Has Called?

My mother insisted.

Somehow or other she had learned of a series of auditions for young children that were taking place in the city centre. The opportunity to be part of the cast in a new production of the musical The Sound of Music to be presented in Belfast's Grand Opera House.

It was the mid-1960s, before any of what became known as 'The Troubles' had broken out in Northern Ireland. I was 9 years old and life was pretty good.

The Grand Opera House is a beautiful Victorian theatre in the centre of Belfast, just recently restored to all its original majestic splendour. For my mother, the idea of her son appearing on stage, dressed in a pair of Lederhosen run up by Sister Maria from the curtains in the Von Trappe family home, would be a dream come true. For me, standing like a right 'tube,'[1] singing Doe a Deer as Friederich or whoever with the other six of my fictional siblings was a potential nightmare of monumental proportions.

I was a working class boy and attended a working class school where even having an unusual name could get you beaten up in the playground. I had a whole bunch of good friends, all of whom were about as far away culturally from the Von Trappe family as you could get. Our ambitions for life involved playing football for the school, playing football for local clubs Linfield or Glentoran, playing football for Manchester United and playing football for Northern Ireland.

That was about it, really. Apart from our immediate ambition to get through each tortuous school day unscathed, as quickly as possible, and then go home. That was an ambition held most obsessively by a lad in my class called Tim. He never spoke to any other kids, never played with anyone else and generally kept himself to himself. I would notice him twice a day. Once, on my way to school when he would shoot past me at lightning pace, running all the way to class.

"Hi, Tim!"

Then once more, as he shot out of the school gates in the afternoon and ran all the way home again, non-stop.

"Bye, Tim!"

Every day, every week, year in and year out. I wonder if he's still running.

Anyway, back to the auditions.

Mothers always win, right? Especially when you're 9 years old. And so it was that I found myself one Saturday morning sitting on a wooden bench alongside a whole bunch of obviously non-working class young ladies and gentlemen, (that's what the auditioning lady called us – I'd never been called a young gentleman in my life), waiting to take the stage and sing *Edelweiss* to three scowling arty types wedged into the comfy seats of the front row of a small theatre in Bedford Street.

I had several plans. The first one was already successful. No one, not one solitary acquaintance, should know about my embarrassing predicament. This I had managed to do, having said nothing to anyone about my mother's plans. My younger brother, Laurence, without any prompting or encouragement from me, never said a word either.

I think he knew how I felt.

My other plans were still a work in process. I would feign a bad cough and, therefore, not sing so well. I would forget my lines. I would sing deliberately out of tune. I would throw up on the stage.

All of these were good workable plans, actually. But, with one major flaw. My mother was with me. Incurring her wrath was only slightly less horrendous than my schoolmates finding out about my performance and making my life unbearable forever. So, reluctantly, when my name was called, I shuffled dolefully on to the stage and sang. Not with enthusiasm or any great aplomb, but reasonably in tune and as quickly as I could.

"Thank you, young Master Mark, that's fine. We'll let you know – NEXT!"

I left the stage mumbling a silent prayer, "Please don't let me win, please don't let me win, PLEASE don't let me win, I'll become a missionary, I'll be good, I'll eat vegetables, please just don't let me win."

I never heard anything from the auditions until about a month or so later when another letter from the company fell through our letterbox at home. It was not addressed to me personally, as it turned out, but instructed that all those involved with the children's cast of *The Sound of Music* should attend the arranged Belfast rehearsals on a specific date.

Who says prayer works?

Crestfallen, when the awful day came I caught the bus into Belfast city centre on my own and trudged reluctantly to the venue, making my way to a signposted rehearsal room in a fairly rundown Arts building.

"Who are you?" said a refined lady who I recognised as one of the aforementioned audition panel.

"I'm Robin Mark, I got a letter."

"Oh, so you're Robin Mark." (Sniggers from the other Von Trappe brats). "Why didn't you come in two weeks ago when we sent you the letter? What's the use of turning up now?"

"I got the letter, here it is, I got it two days ago."

"Not that letter, boy, (apparently no longer a young gentleman). The letter that you received at least three weeks ago that told you you'd been successful in the audition and were to return for a further cast call."

"I never got any letter like that." (I didn't, honestly).

"Well, there's no point hanging around here, is there? The cast is full, as are the understudies (what's an understudy?). You, young gentleman, are a very remiss boy." (what does 'remiss' mean, for goodness sake, woman, talk English). She scowled and gestured with a condescending flick of her head towards the door that, only a few minutes ago, I'd walked through.

Oh, the joy! I can vividly remember bouncing down the stairs from the practice room, bursting through the heavy wooden doors out into the street and running, just like Tim, as fast as I could to the bus stop knowing that my teeth and nose were secure for the time being from my friends and any other rough types in school. I was deliriously happy and I ran like the wind. Maybe that's why Tim runs.

I never did get that letter. Mother was annoyed. The rest of the family ambivalent but slightly bewildered, my brother strangely silent. Although he has never ever said, my immediate thoughts were with my younger brother. To this day I really believe that the letter probably did come, but that, without saying a word and aware of my desperate fears, Laurence probably picked it up from the mat below the letter box, read my name, address and the logo on the envelope, Belfast Upper Class Young Nerds Operatic Chorus (something like that), and quietly but efficiently placed it on the open fire in our living room where it gloriously ignited, burned with vivid yellow flame and eventually disappeared without trace. That lad was obviously inspired.

If there has been a greater act of brotherly love in the whole wide world, I don't know it. I recall he was about seven or eight years old and I around nine. I have never forgotten it. He saved my bacon, that's for sure, and I am eternally grateful.

Who says God doesn't answer prayer?

In the eyes of the world this would probably have been a seminal moment in my life. Young man showing reasonable musical prowess misses out on his big break for stardom and disappears without trace. It's like I got close to the last twelve auditionees in Pop Idol and then just missed the cut. Can you remember any of the folks who just missed the last twelve in Simon Cowell's big talent search this year? No? Don't worry, neither can anyone else.

Not in my eyes was this a problem, of course, but to the onlooker, I probably had pretty much blown it. Any sort of future in the field of the Arts was pretty unlikely.

However, the Bible is full of unlikely people God has called.

That's where the title of this book comes in. Placing the word 'Warrior' with the word 'Poet' may be a traditionally Celtic idea, but in reality we don't often regard or expect those that are trained, armed and kitted out ready for battle to be gifted in creative writing. Nor would we typically expect our artistically gifted friends to be aggressive able warriors ready to charge headlong into the heat of a battlefield. It doesn't seem to make sense and, in the midst of the great spiritual battle for the heart, souls and lives of the men, women and children of the world, you might think that of all the types of people that God could use to make an impact, this WARRIOR POET would certainly not fit the profile.

In fact the Bible is full of ordinary people, who don't quite fit the profile, whom God decides are the men and women or the purposes He wants to fulfil. Ordinary made extraordinary. From the stunningly attractive beauty queen Esther, called for such a time as this to save an entire nation, to the young and insignificant Jeremiah, called to speak God's eternal truth to a lost and disinterested society. From the ex-murderer and poorly spoken Moses to the self-righteous acerbic persecutor of the church, Paul.

The Bible is full of people who were unlikely choices for God's purposes. People essentially minding their own business, just getting by, when God whispers into their ear about some particularly outrageous plan that He wants them to carry out. People like you and me.

This book is about worship. It's about how absolutely important worship is and how, perhaps, it is the highest calling and occupation of the believer. But it's not about excellence of musicianship in played and sung worship. It's not about personalities or individuals, or specially gifted folks, or style, or technique. It's not a how-to book, or a workbook, or a here's-a-service-schedule-that's-bound-to-work type book. It's about how God calls us all to be His worshippers and how, perhaps, every single one of us can, through a deeper understanding of worship, make an impact and a difference in the society in which we live. And it's about those whom God has particularly called for such a time as this, who find themselves at the front of a congregation of God's people with a burning desire to join all their hearts in worship.

So, in the course of this book, I hope to change your mind a little; perhaps cause you to come to realise that you, in fact, may be one of God's WARRIOR POETS called for His good purpose in these days.

I probably should finish this chapter and qualify all that I have said and hope to say by pointing out that I have been drawn to the call of a worship leader in the Church. It's the area of service that God has placed me in, and so it's fair to assume that my perspective on things theological will be heavily biased towards worship. How I got to be a worship leader is another story, which I'll unfold a little more of as we go on. But that is not the important thing. For me, it's all about worship, it's all about Jesus, it's all about the Father, and not really about me at all.

It's all about worship.

Remember that as you read through, and make sure, as you read, that you form your own opinions and ideas in balance with the other great fundamentals of our faith. Read Rob Bell's book Velvet Elvis, for example. Read a book on mission and one on prayer and some of the great works by Erwin McManus. That will keep you in nice balance.

But, for now, take it from me – it's all about worship – the whole thing; everything we are experiencing now in our societies, our communities, our personal and family lives, in my possibly biased opinion, is all about worship.

---

[1] For the word 'tube' (which is Belfast-speak) read geek, nerd, fool or similar.

CHAPTER 2
The Big Question Why?

Before we get to those WARRIOR POETS of the title I need to lay some theological foundations. I appreciate that this may sound a fairly unattractive proposition at this stage, but stick with me. I promise, it will be worth it.

Some time ago I was asked to deliver a series of lectures on the Theology of Worship to a newly-developed undergraduate program at the Source School of Leadership established in our church in Belfast. An honour, for sure, and an invitation I was pleased to take up.

Now, although I am comfortable with my understanding and beliefs in the area of Christian worship, and although I had led worship in my church for almost 20 years, I have to say that, apart from the occasional seminar at a conference or short training program somewhere, I had never delivered a series of studies on the theology of this great subject.

I had read many books on worship, some of which I finished, whilst others were cast aside for use only when I had trouble sleeping at night. And I had read numerous articles and web pages on many aspects of the field. I had, indeed, studied much of the Scripture on the subject through the Old and New Testaments. But I had never sat down and taken time to formulate all my thoughts and understanding into anything like a structured program of learning.

So my first thought and action was to search out and purchase the most recent texts on the Theology of Worship and gain some additional insight before imparting my particular 'knowledge' to the great unlearned masses on our new course. (Seven people turned up.)

Now, I would not wish to incur the wrath of any theologian or publishing house by naming the authors of these worthy volumes, but suffice to say, having worked my way through several hefty texts on worship theology, I was left with one thought. How could a subject so exciting, dramatic and important as the worship of the

Creator of the Universe be rendered so mind-numbingly boring?

Maybe that reaction is what encouraged me to embark on this book, (Lord, please don't let the reader be mind-numbingly bored); but one, hopefully, useful outcome of the study was that it raised a perception in my mind that, whilst the texts covered, commented and criticised different styles of worship practice, they generally failed to answer a very big question.

What is that very big question? "Why Worship?"

Let me put it this way.

Successful author, youth leader and generally all-round decent bloke, Andy Flannigan, came across a list of reasons why we should not worship God in one of the seriously intellectual London-based newspapers in late 2006.

There has been a very recent upsurge in anti-God, anti-Jesus and anti-Christian publications in the past few years. I suppose you could say the resurgence began with the novel, *The DaVinci Code*, and has grown in intensity with other novels and so-called factual books on the lost *Gospels of Judas, Andrew, Mary*, and so on.

I recently visited a Walden's Bookstore in the USA and, on finding the Religion section, discovered that the entire two top shelves were filled with books dedicated to exposing what the writers considered were the myths of Christianity. As a literary and philosophical movement, it is currently riding a wave sustained by the works of celebrated atheists like Richard Dawkins with his text, *The God Delusion*. I suspect that it was one of these authors or a sympathetic reviewer of their work who compiled the list.

Andy read out the list, which I recall was titled, *Seven Reasons not to Worship God*.

Among the list was the writer's opinion that we shouldn't worship God because He's obscure, or because He's unfair, or because He's passive.

However, the one reason that most intrigued me was this: "Because He's egomaniacal and He asks us to."

Why should we not worship God? Answer, "Because He asks us to."

I assume the logic behind this statement is that any thing, being, spiritual force or entity that just straight-out asks you to worship it, must surely be too self-absorbed and demanding to deserve any appropriate response. Any 'god' who entirely expects to receive our unrestricted devotion to the point where they demand to be worshipped, surely must be somehow fundamentally flawed.

For those of us believers, captivated and exposed to the glory of God through the saving work of Jesus Christ, we probably haven't really given this much thought. As the Apostle John says, "We have seen His glory, the glory as of the One and Only, who came from the Father, full of grace and truth" (John 1:14). In light of that revelation, worship is an automatic response.

That Jesus Christ, when encountered, is absolutely the most stunning, enchanting, captivating, and engaging Person you will ever, ever meet, goes without saying. That He, once met, is so high, so incredible, so altogether lovely that to not worship Him totally seems entirely ridiculous, is certain. To know and understand that through Him and in Him we come face to face with God the Father, whose name and character is love, fills us with a joy that has to be expressed in adoration and thanksgiving. That we are restored and filled with His Holy Spirit that cries out to Him, "*Abba*", in sighs too deep for words, is the means by which we give Him glory. This is the truth of worship.

But here's a point to consider.

If you are a believer, since the day you became a Christian and gave your life over to Jesus, what have you been taught and instructed to do?

Pray? Read your Bible? Be honest, trustworthy and diligent in the workplace? Give your money to the work of the local church? Join with, volunteer and get involved in some of the activities of the local church? Actually go to the local church once a week, at least? Follow the Ten Commandments? Be a good member of your family? Witness? Sort your life out?

For sure, these are all good things and important and essential to do. Those of you who became believers in the 60s to 80s were probably given simple written instructions like these after you said the little prayer at conversion, usually in a little pamphlet. Read your Bible, come to church, say your prayers and be good.

You might well be part of a generation who have, probably inadvertently, been told that 'worship' was the singing bit at the start of the service, or the hymns and liturgy running through the service schedule. Perhaps you've come to understand that the meeting on Sunday, or whenever, is 'worship'.

Well, this is all great. But when was the last time you were ever told that one of the most important core activities of your new life was to worship? How often have we been reminded that now we are in relationship with the Creator of the whole world, we need to continue to encounter Him and worship Him and live our entire lives for Him as worshippers? Have you ever been told that all the activities I listed above, and numerous other religious pursuits, are to be carried out as acts of worship and that, in worship, they only become alive and real?

My guess is, not that often. I wonder why?

So for me, perhaps there is some hidden truth and benefit to be found in unfolding the answer to the question posed by that writer in the newspaper. Indeed, what does give God the right to demand our worship? Perhaps if we pursue this it might help our perspective on the place of worship in the Christian's life.

That He requires our worship, totally and without wavering, is a biblical fact.

The very first of the Ten Commandments uses these words: "You shall have no other gods before me." And the second commandment makes it further clear that we are to worship no other god than Him.

Commandments one and two – worship God and none other. It would appear that God does, indeed, fundamentally, demand our worship.

Now the thing is, either there are some very good reasons why God requires or demands this service, or else He is, indeed, as the reactionary atheists propose, not worthy of worship at all.

So, right at the beginning and as best I can, let me attempt to explain why we are required to worship. Because, in all honesty, whatever or whoever demands your worship and your life really must be worthy of that call, does it not? Would we really want to devote our entire life to someone or something who ultimately was never worthy of our commitment in the first place?

To answer this big question, let me firstly try to define what 'worship' is, as I really feel that this will help us take up the challenge of the overall question.

Most of what passes for definitions of worship are, essentially, only definitions of 'how to' worship. If you like, the definitions regard the word 'worship' as a verb and expound on the methodology of our worship. And so we learn that worship is praising, serving our community, serving and loving our families, working in our job as unto the Lord, singing, bowing, lifting up of hands, giving our offerings and tithes, sacrificing, praying, studying the Word, preaching, shouting, offering, playing musical instruments, etc.

These are all actions, or methodologies, to express our worship.

However, in themselves, they cannot define what worship is! The linguistic types among you will notice that most of these active words end in 'ing'; this 'gerund', as it's known, turns the root verbs into nouns, but that noun describes an action or activity. The proper noun 'worship' must be definable in some other way.

Herein lies a fundamental problem within the Church, because when people get upset or wish to assess another church's or individual's worship, they will generally comment on whatever outward expression of worship they can see. They will pass critical judgment on the quality or style of the worship activity that they can observe with their eyes or hear with their ears. That well-worn phrase, "I didn't like the worship today, Pastor" is echoed in many congregations all over the land.

This, of course, makes some sense since man always looks on the outside expression to make an assessment. It's the limit of our capacity and it is, after all, all that we are able to make our judgment on. Of course, God, on the other hand, looks beyond the visible expression and into the heart.

The reality is that no one, absolutely no one, has any right to look on another's outward expression of worship and pass a judgmental comment. Because the outward expression is only as real and sincere and acceptable as the internal condition of the heart that motivates the expression. And that we cannot see.

You see, 'worship' is infinitely deeper and possibly almost indefinable in that context. It's a bit like love. Let me give you an example. Sometimes I buy my wife, Jacqueline, flowers and chocolates. It's an outward expression of love. It's an action that I choose to do which helps me express a deeper feeling. But it does not define my love for her. On another day, I may buy my wife flowers and chocolates and it may have absolutely nothing to do with love at all – it's something else. It's maybe an act of saying sorry, or grovelling, or may be even designed to get something from her! (e.g. Here darling, some chocolates and flowers for you; by the way, I just put a deposit on a Harley Davidson.)

So we can never, ever define love in terms of what we do, for we do not know for sure the motive behind that action, even though we might desperately hope the motive is good.

Neither can we define worship in terms of the action that expresses it.

Many times in seminars the question has been asked that goes something like this: "Robin, we have a whole bunch of people in our church that love the new styles of worship, then we have another bunch who love the old hymns. Both groups can't seem to accept the others preferences and tastes. How do we get over this problem?"

And my answer is often this: "Firstly, that's the wrong question. The issue that you see as a matter of taste in music is not the core issue that is going wrong here. The problem is deeper and more fundamental."

We'll begin our search for the answer to the deeper question of 'Why Worship' near to the start of the Scriptures.

The first mention of an act of worship is in Genesis 4.

I know you've probably heard that the word 'worship', (or one of several words used for worship in the Scriptures) appears much later in Genesis 22 in the passage dealing with Abraham and Isaac and the sacrifice that God required, but the first identifiable act of worship from man to God that takes place in the Bible is in this story of Cain and Abel.

This is very interesting. This action occurs, as the Bible describes, immediately after the Fall and with the second generation of man. So, whatever way you choose to interpret the story, this fascinating portion of Scripture shows us that, after the loss of the close relationship with God as it was meant to be in the garden of Eden, the first action of the next generation of man was an act of worship. Cain and Abel brought an offering to God!

I wonder who told them that they had to do this? Again, trusting in the infinite wisdom and chronology of the Bible, the inference is that, although they were fallen, both sons knew intuitively that it was right to bring an offering of worship to God. There are a few other things about this passage that I want to look at later in this book – but, for now, we have one point to make.

In the previous three chapters of Genesis, neither an act nor a mention of worship is included. Only after the Fall is an 'act' instigated to express what must have been, at one time, a purely natural emotion or relational bond between the Creator and those He created. In other words, there was no need to include an act of worship before the Fall because Adam and Eve's very relationship and proximity to God was what defined their worship. Everything they did in relation to their heavenly Father was pure worship.

Whilst, as we'll discover later, some of the heavenly beings that were in existence were created to express forms or types of worship in a heavenly realm, it appears that the reality was that, before the Fall, the form or action of worship was not necessary. For man, worship itself was simply a normal part of his nature. If you like, similar to, but higher and deeper than, love. Just being in that unbroken close relationship with our Father God was sufficient expression of our worship.

Dostoyevsky in the *Brothers Karamazov* says this, "So long as a man remains free he strives for nothing so incessantly and so painfully as to find someone to worship." D A Carson quotes this short statement and suggests that the Russian author was not wrong to write it. The fact is, we are predisposed to worship.

So, worship is like love. Unfathomable, indeterminable and intrinsically something within us that we will naturally lavish on people, animals and objects around us. We may have ways to express it, but the very nature of love is inexpressible by outward form or ritual. And so it is with worship. Within our very being there is a natural inclination, indeed, a passion, to worship – to give ourselves to someone or something at a level above and beyond love – for love seeks to be requited and hearts are broken when this doesn't happen. But worship gives and expects absolutely nothing in return – worship is given unrequitedly and without seeking personal gain. Worship is higher than love.

Perhaps a simple, if unsatisfactory, example is the worship that someone might lavish on a rock band or artist. You attend the concert and join in the songs; you stand entranced by the person, abilities, skills, looks and qualities of the musicians on stage; you enjoy the experience, though you never meet or exchange words with the stars … they don't even write to you! Yet you make your journey home elated and even more devoted than ever, probably playing more of their music on the way, and still 'worshipping' as you go.

It's not a great example, but it's indicative of the similarities with love, and yet the greater mystery of what is 'worship'.

You give worship because the receiver of that worship is deemed, by you, to be worthy of it. And whatever reaction that receptor has, is irrelevant, you will continue to worship. (Until a better band comes along, of course!)

So why should God, in Himself, actually be in a position to simply require or even demand that this deeply-set essence of our being should be given to Him alone?

Well, I have four reasons for you to think about.

CHAPTER 3

Worship: Why We're Here and Why Things Are As They Are

What we were made for

Why worship? The first reason is this. We worship, fundamentally, because it's why we were made. Some of you may have been brought up in the Presbyterian tradition and will recall the following great statement: "Man's chief end is to glorify God and enjoy Him forever." But for those of you new to the idea that we were made for worship, let me present a biblical proof of it, which may help.

There are a number of coinciding portions in Scripture that illuminate this fact.

Firstly, we need to understand and accept that neither we nor this beautiful planet that we live on were the first thing that God created. God was being a Creator and in the business of 'creating' long before He made this world, man, and everything else in the world. We source the truth of this from the book of Job, the most ancient book in the Bible, when Job, after all his suffering and calling on God for wisdom and understanding in the midst of his trouble, is finally responded to by the Lord. God asks Job a simple question: "Where were you when I formed the earth?"

A tough question, for sure, and one that has really no answer, for neither Job nor any man or woman on earth was with God at that time.

But God continues in His question with a description of that event. He says, "When the morning stars sang together and all the sons of heaven [or angels] shouted for joy?" The 'morning stars' is most properly interpreted as angelic beings as well, though some commentators are happy to regard the reference as to the actual stars in the heaven, but then the physical stars (great big balls of gas) can't really sing. However, the angels, as we know, can really, really sing.

So, by clear inference, there were angelic heavenly beings in existence long before the world and you and I were made.

What was the function of these beings apart from singing during creation? Well, they were designed to worship and serve their Creator. Revelation 5 shows us this in the vast number of angels (100 million, at least) who united to worship the Lamb of God.

That's why they were made. That was their entire function.

There are other elements of God's creation – cherubim and seraphim (types of angels), and four living creatures – described in that same chapter, but their ultimate aim is to give worship to the One who sits on the throne. Revelation 5:13 shows what our ultimate destiny is when it tells us that John then saw "every creature in heaven and earth" singing praises to the Lord as well, as the final point in this act of worship.

So, if God was creating worshipping beings before and up until He created us, it is easy and logical to concur that our creation was just an extension of this creative process. We were made to worship. This planet was made to worship!

And it still goes on.

Our universe is still expanding. Out there in the cosmos, great sun-like stars are contracting, imploding and exploding, and new worlds are being brought into being. All over the world, every second of every day, new life is being brought into being in the human, plant and animal kingdom. All these things are being made to give glory to, to worship, the One who made them. The heavens declare the glory of God, the earth and all that is therein!

We worship God because we, like every other part of God's vast creation, were actually made to worship Him.

Why things are the way they are

The second reason why we worship God is this. The Fall of man and the subsequent battle for his soul is centred around the matter of correct worship. Worship may even be the fundamental issue underpinning this cosmic event.

We all recall the story of the Fall, the presence of the serpent in the garden and the result of man's direct disobedience of God. We know that it's right there in the first chapters of Genesis that we find the biblical explanation for both our current personal state and the state of the world in which we live.

However, the Bible presents us with corresponding passages and related portions of Scripture that fully explain the circumstances and the events that took place in advance of this seminal moment for mankind. And, again, I'd like to suggest to you that at the core of the motivation for these events was the issue of worship.

Actually, an interesting aside occurs. I received some book tokens as a birthday gift recently and decided to buy the Richard Dawkins book, The God Delusion. Dawkins is a fervent atheist and decidedly anti-God and, by association, somewhat anti-Christian. (That's what you call an understatement, by the way.) My reasons for purchasing the book were many, but most fundamentally, I wanted to see if, reading with an open mind balanced by what I believe is true about life on earth, I could take on the challenges that Dawkins raises and deal with them satisfactorily in the context of my belief in Christ.

In effect, it wasn't too difficult. It's not that great a book. In fact, apart from his writing in his own scientific field, it's pretty hopeless. And one of the most intriguing portions of the book occurs in chapter seven when Dawkins takes several pages to express his inability to fathom the God whose first two commandments relate to worship and how angry He is when that worship is given to another. Dawkins is entirely bewildered by the thought, unable to comprehend the circumstances or the logic. He cannot get his head around the idea.

You see, even he, as a committed atheist, has stumbled upon the fact that somehow this unfathomable concept of 'worship' is important to God and also in our lives and has a significantly deeper and more mysterious impact than at first appears.

Anyway, back again to the passage. The first hint of the cosmological impact of worship and the garden of Eden is in Isaiah 14:12-15:

How you have fallen from heaven, O morning star, son of the dawn! You have been cast down to the earth, you who once laid low the nations! You said in your heart, 'I will ascend to heaven; I will raise my throne above the stars of God; I will sit enthroned on the mount of assembly, the utmost heights of the sacred mountain. I will ascend above the tops of the clouds; I will make myself like the Most High.' But you are brought down to the grave, to the depths of the pit.

This is a fairly well-known passage, but without reading anything into it other than what it clearly states, (we want to try and keep to the expressed text of the Scriptures and not speculate in any way), two or three matters emerge.

The term 'morning star' tells us that we are talking about a heavenly being, or an angel, right? We just established that from Job 38. Those 'morning stars' were the sons of heaven or angelic beings. 'Son of the dawn' as a title tells us that the being was important or at least significant enough in having a specific title. This angelic being fell or was cast down from heaven, even to the grave. We identify him as Lucifer or Satan. Christ Himself makes the statement in Luke 10:18 that He "saw Satan fall like lightning from heaven", so we get the overall picture.

Verses 13 and 14 tell us why the event of the angelic fall happened. Most of us will have been taught that the issue was pride, and that it was the pride of his heart that caused this 'son of the dawn' to fall. Now, for sure, pride was one of the issues that had a bearing on the events that followed, and we'll see this clarified in a parallel passage coming up.

However, I'd like to suggest that the real issue here was much more relevant and closer to worship. As these verses read, the matter was one of ambition, rather than possession. Pride is normally associated with a pleasure, often selfish and self-absorbed, in something we have already attained or already possess. There's no doubt, as we shall see, that Satan was proud of his attributes and beauty, but the matters discussed in verses 13 and 14 are with regard to a place of stature and importance that this fallen angel sought to achieve. It was a selfish ambition, rather than pride. Or, if you like, it was a wrong and selfish ambitiousness built upon pride.

To quote again, Satan's words: "I will ascend to heaven; I will raise my throne above the stars of God; I will sit enthroned on the mount of assembly, on the utmost heights of the sacred mountain. I will ascend above the tops of the clouds; I will make myself like the Most High."

To what did this ambition pertain? According to the passage, he wanted to sit enthroned on the mount, in the heights of the sacred assembly; he wanted to be like God.

In other words, Satan wanted to receive worship rather than give it. Satan's fall was all to do with who or what is the ultimate recipient of our worship. Therefore he was cast down. He who was made to worship sought to be worshipped, rather than give worship. His issue was with worship, and his actions on earth have all been about worship ever since that day.

Whatever your understanding of the first few chapters of Genesis, this event described in the book of Isaiah must have happened either during the creation of the earth, or just before that event was completed, or perhaps a long time before this when the "earth was without form and void". But, whatever our understanding of the chronology, this is why Satan, described as 'the serpent' by the author of Genesis, was present and instrumental at the Fall. He was after man's worship.

As confirmation and further enlightenment we can go to another related passage in Ezekiel 28:11-17:

The word of the LORD came to me: Son of man, take up a lament concerning the king of Tyre and say to him: This is what the Sovereign LORD says: 'You were the model of perfection, full of wisdom and perfect in beauty. You were in Eden, the garden of God; every precious stone adorned you: ruby, topaz and emerald, chrysolite, onyx and jasper, sapphire, turquoise and beryl. Your settings and mountings were made of gold; on the day you were created they were prepared. You were anointed as a guardian cherub, for so I ordained you. You were on the holy mount of God; you walked among the fiery stones. You were blameless in your ways from the day you were created till wickedness was found in you. Through your widespread trade you were filled with violence, and you sinned. So I drove you in disgrace from the mount of God, and I expelled you, O guardian cherub, from among the fiery stones. Your heart became proud on account of your beauty, and you corrupted your wisdom because of your splendour.'

In this passage Satan is equated to the King of Tyre, an island capital in Phoenicia or modern-day Lebanon that was overrun and conquered by the Babylonian Empire. So, whilst the prophet is warning the King of Tyre regarding the future of his city, the earthly physical king is used as a portrayal of the circumstances of a spiritual king at work on the earth.

It's clear that it places him in Eden in verse 13, and in verse 14 it indicates again how important or senior he was. 'A guardian cherub', no less. Again, some theologians have taken this to mean his possible equivalence of status to the archangels Michael and Gabriel, but avoiding any speculative approach, we at the very least are made aware of his importance.

The rest of the passage mirrors Isaiah in unfolding the fall of this beautiful angel.

And so, the one who sought to usurp God from that place of ultimate worship was cast down from heaven, along with what Revelation calls in a further parallel passage, a third of the angels (cf. Revelation 12:7-9).

And, on the earth, his purpose has never changed. He began by usurping God's authority, spoiling the relationship between man and God, and seeking worship for himself, and he continues to do so. The proliferation all around us of gods, religions, deities, and the acts associated with their existence is evidence enough of his work on the earth. But he shows his true colours again in the New Testament, in the story of Christ's temptation.

Matthew 4 shows us that Satan has never changed. His temptations to Jesus, when the Lord was at a low physical ebb, hungry, tired and still in the wilderness, are evidence enough. Satan challenges Him first in the area of provision and trust in the relational power of God to provide; then he challenges His understanding of who He really is and whether He needs to prove His trust in His Heavenly Father's hand in His life. Finally, Satan nails the question as he shows Jesus all the kingdoms of the world – "I will give you all their authority and splendour, for it has been given to me, and I can give it to anyone I want to. So if you worship me, it will all be yours" (Luke 4:5-7). In other words, "Here's my final offer, Jesus. I have all this now, all that You can see is worshipping me – if You want it back, You can have it – all You've got to do is worship me instead!"

Three questions to the Son of God: Can God do what He says He can do? Is God to be trusted? Who will You worship?

How staggering that these three matters are what sealed our fate in the first place, when the same fallen angel was there in the Garden posing exactly the same questions to Adam and Eve. Is God to be trusted? Will He do what He says He'll do? Why don't you do what I say and usurp the place of God in your life, why not worship me?

The battle, still raging on this earth, is about worship. Christ's resistance was about worship, and His salvation to restore that broken Eden relationship is fundamentally also about worship.

OK, I may be really biased, but here's the thing. Forget your 10 step program, forget the pursuit of earthly security and provision, forget all the trappings of being in church, forget committees and programs and timetabling endeavours and concerts and services. Whilst these are very worthy and probably essential areas of church life, the reality is – in the great scheme of things – this is all about worship.

Thus the second reason 'why worship' is this. Worship is the very reason why this fallen creation is where it is, in the midst of a spiritual war for the souls of men. Jesus refused to usurp the worship of His Father and we need to understand how central worship is in the battle for the salvation of the world.

CHAPTER 4

Two More Reasons Why: Ownership and Blessing

God's Possession

The third reason, 'Why worship?' has to do with ownership.

So, your very good friend and billionaire Bill Gates calls you up one night, (we live in hope) and says: "Hey, guess what, I just bought myself a new painting by that guy Van Gogh. You know, one ear short of a pair, ginger beard and all. Cost me millions and millions of dollars. I've built a special room in my home for it and I'd like you to come round for a private viewing – what do you say?"

"Why I'd love to, Bill!"

So you hop on your bicycle, pedal round to Bill's house, go through security, the valet guy rides off to park your bicycle and, in the fulness of time, you find yourself in the beautifully lit and specially constructed, climate controlled room where the sole object in the room is there mounted on the wall ... the painting.

And it is stunning!

What do you say?

Well, you probably say something like: "What an absolutely stunning Van Gogh!"

Now, old Bill might protest, "Well, it's mine now."

But the reality is, no matter how many millions of dollars he had to pay out and no matter what special enclosure he built to house it, one thing never changes – it is not a 'Bill Gates' painting.

It's a Van Gogh.

For no matter who owns the piece temporarily at any time, the painting will always be known by its author and the one who really has 'ownership'. It will always be a Van Gogh painting.

In the very same way, you and I are God's possession. All of us. Even if you've been forced to read this book by a Christian friend and don't have any relationship or interest in Christ or God or anything. He made us, He crafted us, He formed us. He is the celestial craftsman at work in our lives. He is the great artist of our destiny. No matter who lays claim to our heart, no matter who thinks they own us, in His eyes we are His special possession. We are His masterpiece.

That's why He demands our worship and why He can demand it. This is why He is a jealous God and our misplaced worship causes Him such distress and anger.

Because, fundamentally, He owns us.

Many of you may know that I wrote a song called *Days of Elijah* some years back which has become kind of popular. There's a chapter in this book, near the end, which tells the story of that song and how it came to be composed (if you're interested).

About once a month for the past seven or eight years I will get at least one person from somewhere in the world writing to me to tell me about a 'third verse' they have written. I've had a few emails and letters that proposed a third and a fourth verse and even one with three extra verses! My wife estimates that, if I'd kept them, we would have somewhere in the region of 40 to 50 extra verses. Which would make for a very big song, don't you think?

The folks that do this are very sweet and usually ask my thoughts or opinions. Most time I try to write back, commend them for their efforts, and explain that I've received so many different additional verses that I can neither make a judgment on them nor incorporate them into the song. Sometimes I pass on little pieces of advice on copyright law etc., but not that often since the day I received a really angry response back from one source. Which is another story.

But often, way down deep in the pit of my stomach, there's another little voice of response trying to be heard. And this little voice says, "This is my song, I wrote it. If you want to write a verse, then go and write your own song!"

Yes, I know, shameful, eh?

Like a good Christian boy, I used to try and subdue this little reactionary voice as I assumed it was the old flesh man rearing its ugly head again in selfishness.

And then someone passed on a little gem of a thought. "Robin," they said, "God is our great Creator, He made us in His image and therefore we are all made with creative ability, from the least to the greatest. What you are experiencing is the Creator's possessiveness, that's all. You are passionate and possessive of your own creation."

Folks, (as my friend Andrew would say when he preaches), here's the truth. Those of you reading this who have ever painted a painting, written a story, made a clay model, sculpted in stone, written a song, composed a musical score – whatever you have done in creativity – should someone pay you a fortune for it and mount it in a shop window in 5th Avenue, New York with a vast price tag on it, whenever you walk past that window and look in at that display, you will think to yourself, "Hey, that's mine!" It will still be your work, your making, your creation. And nothing, absolutely nothing, will ever change that.

We are God's handiwork, God's possession, and God's creation. He can require our worship without any doubt or sense of selfishness or capriciousness. We are His! That's why it breaks His heart when we choose to extract ourselves from the Father Creator's loving grasp and go elsewhere to worship and give ownership to other gods. This is why He gets jealous.

One more story on this third reason, 'Why worship?' It's not a great illustration, but it may help you understand this more fully.

I used to work in a Technical College. In America and other parts of the world you might call it a Community College, somewhere between school and university where people learn skills like carpentry and metalwork and car mechanics and all that. I taught a subject called Building Science and Civil Engineering to a lovely bunch of guys.

But as many of you will know who have been in teaching at some point in your life, sometimes when folks are off sick or otherwise unable to come into work, you get to cover and watch over a class for which you probably have no qualifications or knowledge or skill whatsoever.

And so it was that one fine day my good friend and colleague, Alex Muirhead, was off ill. His class that morning was carpentry for a special needs group of boys aged about 15 or 16 from the Special Care School up the road.

I had never taught a special needs group, let alone carpentry. But, never fear, said the departmental head, the technician 'Tommy' would be on hand to get the class started. So off I went to teach.

In the room around a dozen eager faces watched as Tommy the technician set down one piece of timber, about 300mm long and 50mm by 12mm in cross section, at each workbench, (that's a foot by two inches by a half inch for you Americans out there). Then he showed how they would fix the wood in the vice, use the saw (which he also had placed on each bench) to cut the timber in half on a pre-drawn line, and then take some sandpaper and smooth the saw cut off. That was it. Saw the wood in half and then smooth it.

After the demonstration Tommy turned to me with an expression that said, 'Over to you, sonny.'

I duly addressed the class. "OK," I chimed, "now it's your turn."

And so, off they went. I sat up at the front desk, glancing occasionally in their direction to ensure all was well. Saws flashed furiously back and forth as the boys set about their task.

(Actually, as an aside, when Alex the proper carpentry teacher returned a few days later he told me he'd never given that particular class anything sharper than a tube of glue to work with, for safety reasons. The fact that no limbs were lost when I was in charge is a minor miracle! Praise the Lord!)

I carried on marking some papers, or whatever, and generally ignored what was going on. Until, sometime into the class, there came an unworldly wailing from the centre of the room.

Oh no, I thought, now what. Has someone just lost a finger?

Two or three benches back from the front desk a young Downs Syndrome boy was inconsolably sobbing over his work, which lay in front of him on the workbench. His friend, who was finding it a bit amusing it has to be said, explained simply what the problem was.

"His work got messed up and it's ruined."

The saw cut wasn't straight, his attempts to rectify it halfway through had zigzagged across the wood and no amount of sanding would smooth out the jagged edges of the job.

That was all, but he was devastated. What was intended to be a beautiful work of craftsmanship got all messed up, and it broke this little creator's heart.

It's not a great example, I suppose, but at that point a thought on God's creation flashed through my mind. It started as perfect and pure, a creative act of unsurpassed beauty. But then it got messed up and ruined. God saw what happened to His glorious creation and it broke His heart.

But not only that, it moved Him to set about that wonderful pursuit of the hearts of men to restore our relationship and worship through His Son.

It's for our own good

The fourth reason why we worship is that it's for our own good.

God demands our worship, amongst all the other reasons we have mentioned, because it is ultimately good for us and opens the path of blessing to us.

Of course, that's not a reason to have on our hearts when we come to worship. Whenever we get the impression that worship is a means to receive rather than give we essentially compromise the very nature of worship. So we need to be careful with this thought.

However, I honestly believe the Scriptures tell us that this is the case. So long as it is not the reason for our worship, a real by-product of our worship is blessing.

To look at this very important idea in detail, I need to skip forward in the Scriptures to the book of Kings and look at some interesting passages that seem to suggest that not only is worship right, proper, and fundamental to who we are, but worship may well be one of the keys to God's blessing, not just on us, but on the communities in which we live.

Anyway, do you like soap operas?

CHAPTER 5

Kings and Nations

Exactly. I wonder if you're a fan of soap operas on television?

In the USA most studio-based television soap operas are daytime shows for afternoon viewers, but in the UK and Ireland it's possible to settle down at around 5:30pm and watch soap operas unfolding all night long. For about 3 or 4 hours every evening a bit of careful manipulation of the remote control can see you follow the lives of ordinary folk in London's Albert Square, Northern England's Coronation Street, Australian suburban avenues, American hospitals, and just about any other environment you care to think of.

Jackie, my wife, loves them. I can just about tolerate one or two at most. But for millions of people, the soap operas are a not to be missed televisual experience every night of the week. Of course, the main attraction of this regular entertainment provision is the ebb and flow of the lives, and deaths, of fictional characters and situations into which the viewing public become immersed and absorbed.

We all love a good story.

We all love a bit of adventure; we love a mystery; we love to contrast the mundane and the ordinary with the cruel twists of fate and startling revelations which make the soap opera sparkle. We all love to see a reflection, albeit slightly warped, of our own lives acted out on screen.

One of the greatest true soap operas in literature is a majestic story spanning 500 years or more and told in the biblical books of 1st and 2nd Kings. It features the lives of rulers and servants, tribes and individuals, nations and neighbours in a tempestuous roller coaster ride of mammoth proportions charting the history of the nation and kings of Israel.

At the heart of the story is worship.

In fact, on careful review, the entire story is hinged and structured on worship. If we look close enough we'll find that the very health, welfare and prosperity of God's people rested and depended on their worship.

At the beginning of the first book of Kings we enter a period in the history of Israel where David, at his death, passes the rule of his strong, godly kingdom to his wise and benevolent son, Solomon. The twelve tribes of Israel are united and secure, fully established in the promised land and living lives of provision and plenty.

The circumstances are described in 1 Kings 4:20-34. Here's a selection from that passage describing life in Israel at that time,

> The people of Judah and Israel were as numerous as the sand on the seashore; they ate, they drank and they were happy. And Solomon ruled over all the kingdoms from the River to the land of the Philistines, as far as the border of Egypt. These countries brought tribute and were Solomon's subjects all his life . . . . Solomon's daily provisions were thirty cors of fine flour and sixty cors of meal, ten head of stall-fed cattle, twenty of pasture-fed cattle and a hundred sheep and goats, as well as deer, gazelles, roebucks and choice fowl. For he ruled over all the kingdoms west of the River, from Tiphsah to Gaza, and had peace on all sides. During Solomon's lifetime Judah and Israel, from Dan to Beersheba, lived in safety, each man under his own vine and fig tree.

That last phrase basically means everyone had all their needs met, had sufficient to eat and enough to drink and lived in peace and harmony with their neighbours. Their ruler was the wisest man in the world and had tribute brought to him by the leaders of the surrounding kingdoms. They were at total peace with each other, their neighbours and their God. We are talking as near as possible to Utopia for the nation of Israel. Life was just about as good as it gets.

But now let's read a parallel passage a few hundred years later in the book of 2 Kings 25:1-11

So in the ninth year of Zedekiah's reign, on the tenth day of the tenth month, Nebuchadnezzar king of Babylon marched against Jerusalem with his whole army. He encamped outside the city and built siege works all around it. The city was kept under siege until the eleventh year of King Zedekiah. By the ninth day of the fourth month the famine in the city had become so severe that there was no food for the people to eat. Then the city wall was broken through, and the whole army fled at night through the gate between the two walls near the king's garden, though the Babylonians were surrounding the city. They fled toward the Arabah, but the Babylonian army pursued the king and overtook him in the plains of Jericho. All his soldiers were separated from him and scattered, and he was captured. He was taken to the king of Babylon at Riblah, where sentence was pronounced on him. They killed the sons of Zedekiah before his eyes. Then they put out his eyes, bound him with bronze shackles and took him to Babylon. On the seventh day of the fifth month, in the nineteenth year of Nebuchadnezzar king of Babylon, Nebuzaradan commander of the imperial guard, an official of the king of Babylon, came to Jerusalem. He set fire to the temple of the LORD, the royal palace and all the houses of Jerusalem. Every important building he burned down. The whole Babylonian army, under the commander of the imperial guard, broke down the walls around Jerusalem. Nebuzaradan the commander of the guard carried into exile the people who remained in the city, along with the rest of the populace and those who had gone over to the king of Babylon.

Beginning from the start of the book of Kings and Solomon's utopian society, we have now come to a seminal moment in the nation's history. It had been a long slow but significant decline into chaos for God's chosen people. By this time the overall original nation of Israel had split into two and the northern portion of the nation, which consisted of the majority of the twelve tribes and is, itself, called Israel, was first to be overthrown by the peoples that surrounded them.

The passage in 2 Kings 25 describes the last days of the kingdom of Judah, the smaller southern counterpart.

These sombre and frightening words describe just about the most desperate situation in the Bible. It is a staggering and pitiful contrast to the early chapters in Kings. If we were reading the two books of Kings like a novel and had no understanding or knowledge of how things developed after this event, we would probably consider this passage to be the very sad end of the previously unfolded story.

This final stage, where the remnant of the once great nation of Israel are taken off into captivity, perhaps feels a little like one of those sad endings rejected by a movie audience who are gathered for the preliminary screening of a new film. You know the sort of thing, where the director and the studio executives 'try out' differing final scenarios to gauge audience response before releasing the final cut. Well, for me, this ending would get rejected right away! It's just too hard to bear in the circumstances. In fact, and incredibly, it seems to be the apparent end of the 'promise' that God gave to His people, broken and destroyed because of their attitude and heart.

What brought this once great nation to its knees?

To give you some further idea of the magnitude of the impact, at the beginning of the story this people group are as "numerous as the sand on the seashore" (1 Kings 4:20). In all probability they numbered several million people. A fairly substantial nation.

Towards the end of this part of the story of Israel, in the book of Ezra, the population numbers are counted again when a remnant of God's chosen people eventually get to return to their homeland. Only somewhere between 20,000 and 40,000 are left of the original bloodline! From several million to a few thousand and, but for

God's grace, almost totally obliterated from the earth.

What, indeed, brought this great nation to its knees?

Well, the Bible never fails us in our search for answers and clues to the events of history.

In the middle of the second book of Kings the writer laments the falling of the northern kingdom of Israel and takes the time to explain to you, the reader, why such a catastrophic fall from grace had occurred.

We've had a few passages in a row in this part of our story, but here is the last one for now from 2 Kings 17:7-17,

All this took place because the Israelites had sinned against the Lord their God who had brought them out of Egypt. They worshipped other gods and followed the practices of the nation the Lord had driven out before them. As well as the practices that the kings of Israel had introduced, the Israelites secretly did things against the Lord their God that were not right. From watchtower to fortified city they built themselves high places in all their towns. They set up sacred stones and Asherah poles on every high hill and under every spreading tree. At every high place they burned incense as the nations whom the Lord had driven out before them had done. They did wicked things that provoked the Lord to anger. They worshipped idols though the Lord had said, 'You shall not do this.' The Lord warned Israel and Judah through all his prophets and seers, 'Turn from your evil ways, Observe My commands and decrees, in accordance with the entire law that I commanded your fathers to obey and that I delivered to you through My servants the prophets.' But they would not listen and were as stiff-necked as their fathers who did not trust in the Lord their God. They rejected His decrees and the covenant He had made with their fathers and the warnings He had given them. They followed worthless idols and themselves became worthless. They imitated the nations around them although the Lord had ordered them, 'Do not do as they do' and they did the things the Lord had forbidden them to do. They forsook all the commands of the Lord their God and made for themselves two idols cast in the shape of calves and Asherah poles. They bowed down to all the starry hosts and they worshipped Baal. They sacrificed their sons and daughters in the fire. They practised divination and sorcery and sold themselves to do evil in the eyes of the Lord, provoking Him to anger.

The writer, probably the prophet Jeremiah, identifies all the areas where the Israelites had fallen and brought about their own destruction. In the verses quoted above, we read of all the things that they did as a people, the consequence of which was their final downfall.

Different translations of the Bible give minor variations to the points that the writer expounds, but of the 14 or so specific detailed examples of the Israelites turning from God and sinning stated in the New International Version translation above, 13 relate, specifically and clearly, to worship.

Read through the passage again. I have highlighted the relevant statements in the text for you. Where the writer identifies a particular activity equating to their sin, 13 times out of 14, it is specifically to do with worship. Sometimes he uses phrases like 'reject', 'disobey', and 'did evil' as general terms, but where he specifically describes a wrong act committed by the Israelites, almost all the examples have to do with worship.

Now, in the world that we live in, we still understand the scientific concept of cause and effect. Every action brings about a reaction. You reap what you sow. Any action will result in an impact or a change in the object upon which the action is taking place.

In a passage like 2 Kings 17, this raises an important truth.

If someone were to show the reason for a circumstance occurring, in this case the fall of a nation, and can attribute almost 95% of the reasons for that occurrence to a single cause, (in this case wrong worship) – then we have, essentially, established a truth. If this were a scientific experiment and the experiment was found to yield the same result 13 times out of 14, we would describe it as a law, a rule, an almost incontrovertible truth.

And that 'truth' is this: if you worship other gods and give yourself to them, you will, as a consequence, suffer ruin.

Beyond a shadow of doubt, at the core of the fall of the Northern Kingdom, and their principal 'sin', was a failure to give God the worship He required. There is, again, little further doubt that when the southern portion of the kingdom was eventually overthrown, this issue of worship was also at the core of their demise.

What brought this once great nation to its knees?

False worship.

Is this a measure of the importance of worship? That an entire nation's prosperity and security was dependent on their worship? That their future was bound up in presenting true worship to their God? That their success and very existence owed everything to worship?

If this is true, then futile and pointless arguments about style, form, tradition and music that seem to absorb so much of our time on worship these days start to pale into insignificance when compared to the outcome that befell a nation that had ceased to worship their God.

It is true, is it not, that today, the spiritual health of God's Church is entirely dependent on its heart of worship?

I think we would all accept that to a greater or lesser degree.

When I began to lead worship in the early days it was common to encounter groups of believers, or churches, who preferred not to sing what were described as 'modern' hymns. I never had a problem with this, nor should anyone, because if it were just a matter of taste or musical preference then it would be of no consequence, right? As long as the heart of worship was good, there would be no problem.

However, the reality, unfortunately, was that it wasn't just a choice between style and form, it was a choice of tradition over something that God was doing in the body. And so, today, there are many churches which made a decision to follow a traditional form or style who are slowly but surely ebbing away in numbers and impact on their communities. Of course, there are vibrant dynamic churches with traditional styles of worship, but these are churches whose decision on style is only a matter of taste – these are churches that worship the Lord 'in spirit and truth' using the glorious hymn writers and liturgy composers of the past. Taste, style and form will never be the real issue. The heart of worship is the core.

So we would generally accept that the success of a church is directly correlated to the worshipping heart in that church, however that worship is expressed.

However, is it possible that this statement might also be true of a community, a neighbourhood, a city or town or a region? Is it even possible that the very health of an entire nation comes down to who or what they choose to place at the centre of their lives? Is it possible that the very existence of your nation or my nation, or any nation under heaven, might depend on their worship?

I believe it is possible, and I believe this passage is in the book of Kings to make it clear to us how important worship is and another reason why we worship.

One summer I visited a church in Vancouver, Canada pastored by a wonderful man named Barney Coombes.

Barney has been an influencer and mentor to many people throughout the recent history of the renewal movement in the Church. His current congregation is based in one of the ethnically diverse parts of Vancouver and there is a continual inflow of peoples from 'every tribe and nation' to the area. It would seem an appropriate place for a Christian witness.

I had the pleasure of visiting the church a few years back and one of his assistant pastors told me this story.

One evening a Chinese lady, not long in the city, called at the church when one of the members just happened to be busying himself outside the front foyer. She approached him and said, in broken English, that she wanted to know about Jesus.

In the course of the next few moments conversation, before taking her inside the church to a ministry team, he happened to ask her why she had come with such a direct request. Her answer was simple, probably an over-simplification of the reality of things, but at the same time, most profound.

She had surmised as she looked at her own country at that time and the other countries of the world, that those that knew Jesus seemed to be the most prosperous, peaceful, caring and free societies. She opined that Christian countries seemed secure and open whilst those that followed other belief systems appeared oppressive, restrictive, closed and troubled. So she wanted to find out about this Jesus who was able to make even entire nations 'good'. Now, I stress, this was not the self-righteous opinion of a westerner looking out on the other nations of the world. This was a lady seeking the truth, explaining her motivation, as she saw it.

She makes an interesting, thought provoking statement, doesn't she?

For me, coming from Northern Ireland and having been part of a 'Christian' society which for many years has suffered so much strife, sectarianism and pain, you might feel that we're, at best, the exception that proves the rule; or, at worst, an example of the very opposite of her opinion. But throughout the troubled years in our country I need you to know that it was the fervent prayers and sacrificial actions of many, many good people that have brought us, with God's grace, to the place we are now.

And perhaps in our 21st Century cynicism many of us are musing this very moment on matters relating to military arsenals, armies, excessive wealth, greed and abuse which appears to be at the core of most of the nations that form our western society.

But she was a simple woman making a simple, though possibly, profound point. It makes you think, doesn't it?

And even those weaknesses and flaws I have identified above, which are so common in our society, get addressed by God in the books of Isaiah and Amos, again in the context of worship. One of the chapters following will look at that very thing. We will see how even this aspect of the life of an individual and a nation comes right down to who we 'worship'.

And so I'll say it again, who and how we worship has an absolute influence, not only on our own lives, but on the churches and communities, cities and towns, nations and peoples that we live and minister with.

One more reason to believe this is a core truth and the fourth reason why we should worship God, and then we'll move on.

I am afraid I am not a proper musician. (You'd never have guessed, right?)

I've never been properly trained in music theory and practice. Worse still, though I try to read and learn as much as possible, I have no formal training in creative writing or literature beyond the age of sixteen when I managed to scrape a pass in my school studies. Even worse still, (and a source of several geek or nerd jibes amongst my loving musician friends), I am a mathematician. All my qualifications and studies are in pure and applied maths of one sort or another.

I actually love numbers and sums and math and numerical problem solving. How sad is that?

Someone asked me recently how I manage to go to the gym (occasionally), and not get bored stupid by the repetitive tasks. Well, truth is, I count! I play little number games in my head whilst I climb the stair-master, or cross train or row, to keep me amused whilst I'm expending all that effort and never getting anywhere!

So I believe in the power of numbers and statistics! How's this:

If God says it once, it's important.
If He says it twice, it's very important.
If He says it again and again, it is absolutely fundamental.

Fortunately, many of the Bible writers share my enthusiasm for things mathematical! They use numbers to indicate the relative importance of instructions and information in the Scriptures. Here are a few examples: Amos 1:3, 6, 9 etc. "For three sins and for four." Matthew 12:40, "For as Jonah was three days and three nights in the belly of a huge fish, so the Son of Man will be three days and three nights in the heart of the earth." Proverbs 30:18, "There are three things I cannot understand, four are too amazing for me!"

See what I mean?

For all you mathematicians out there, here's the rub.

Leaving aside the book of Kings for the moment, in the book of Exodus, God gives Moses Ten Commandments (Exodus 20:1-17).

Of those Ten Commandments two specifically relate to where we direct our worship, and they come first! The third and fourth indirectly refer to a worship lifestyle in not misusing His name and setting aside time in our week to give to Him alone. For good measure the last commandment of the ten is essentially a heart/worship issue – don't want the things that your neighbour has. In other words, don't be desirous of things, but be desirous of God.

That's five out of ten, or 50%, or half the commandments are related to worship. Four of them precede the 'right living' commandments.

Worship is fundamental to everything that we are. Who we worship and how we worship has great effect on our lives and the lives of those around us.

And so we come to this.

If this is the case, then we need to be sure that our worship is actually the type of worship that God wants. The type that He demands. We need to be sure that our hearts are right before Him. It cannot be about what songs we write or sing, it cannot just be about liturgy, style, rhythm, words, poetry, location, visuals, or any of the many and varied methodologies that we use in corporate church times.

It must be something deeper. But it is desperately important.

All of you singers, all you musicians, all you artists, all you businessmen, all you shop workers, all you children, all you parents, all you worshippers – let's look again at this subject of worship with this premise in mind. How we worship is going to affect our churches, communities, towns, cities and nations. That's a measure of its importance.

And if this is so, did God leave us at the fourth chapter of Genesis (where we began our study) to our own devices, out of the Garden and out of His presence, without letting us know how important worship was?

I don't think so. In fact, I believe that from that point and to this day, God is still pursuing the worshipping heart of man.

CHAPTER 6

Worship:
The Pursuit of God [1]

The first few chapters of this book have attempted to answer the question, Why we worship.

I proposed four reasons:

1. It's what we were made for.
2. It's what this world is all about.
3. It's because of the ownership of God.
4. It's because it is for our own good and that of the communities around us.

If these are true, then God is surely inclined to remind His Church of the importance of worship on a regular basis throughout its history. In that respect we would expect to find recurring worship resurgences and renaissance. It isn't hard to see how, particularly in music and song, worship has been highlighted throughout the history of the Church.

Sometimes I fear for the Church when, in the midst of this time of restoration of worship, we have commentators undermining whatever the current wave of worship is; record and music industries taking advantage of the genre; people, who should know better, using phrases such as 'worship wars' in articles, books and from the pulpit when they refer not to any spiritual battle, but to some petty disagreement over musical style, (now that has to be offensive to the Father, surely?).

When Isaac Watts was composing his great songs of praise in the 18th Century, writing timeless works like When I Survey and How Sweet the Name of Jesus Sounds, he was of course pilloried by the established church structures for his beliefs and his style. Indeed, he suffered the term 'versifier' from critics as a measured insult to what was perceived as his poetic shortcomings. It's hard to believe that now, but the same attitude and commentary is not uncommon today, levelled against many of the current writers and composers of worship music.

Of course, everyone is allowed their opinion, and to express it. And I personally would be first to admit that not all my songs are classical examples of the form.

However, the only proper explanation I can see for the kind of discord that can arise is that someone else knows how crucial true worship is to the heart of God and the future of mankind and is trying to mess it all up as much as possible. That 'someone else' who began that very same discord, long ago in the Garden.

But, if worship is so important in the context of the Church, in our personal lives and even in our world or our nations, then you might expect God to say something about it pretty close to the start of His Book. The importance of worship in the Church and the world we live in might be reflected in how soon the subject and nature of worship is presented in the Bible.

Sure enough, right where we left off after the Fall, in Genesis 4, a series of events and stories gives us an immediate understanding of, again, how important worship is. How important it is to us, and how important it is to God.

Indeed, in the context of a fallen society, how worship is a key to restoration.

By way of reminder, Genesis 1-2 tell the story of creation and the beauty of all that was made by God, including the relationship that man enjoyed with his heavenly Father. The 'how it was meant to be' scenario.

Genesis 3 then tells the awful story of the Fall and the expulsion from the Garden and the seeming end of that relationship.

Within these first three chapters we are presented with what was meant to be after the creation and, unfortunately, what resulted due to man's wilful disobedience. These chapters have formed the core of our understanding of the redemptive process fulfilled by Christ's sacrifice and set the stage, not only for the remainder of the Bible, but for history itself. Many of you will know that the writer, pictorially and prophetically, speaks of Christ in Genesis 3:15 and of the battle that was to ensue for the hearts of men. "He will crush your head [Satan] and you will strike His heel."

Genesis 4 follows on from this terrible event, forever known as 'the Fall of man' and, as you might expect, contains stories cataloguing events which mirror much of the trouble that has beset all our societies throughout time. It includes the banishment from the Garden, murder, dissent and the beginnings of strife and enmity for the human race.

It is a sad and horrid catalogue of the downward spiral into which man inevitably falls. It certainly does not appear to be a particularly uplifting chapter and you might wonder about my earlier assertion that it has much to teach us about the importance of worship. In fact, commentators and theologians use the word 'cursed' or 'accursed' when they talk of the characters and events that fill this chapter.

Genesis 4:1-15 says,

Adam lay with his wife Eve and she became pregnant and gave birth to Cain. She said 'With the help of the Lord I have brought forth a man.' Later she gave birth to his brother Abel. Now Abel kept flocks and Cain worked the soil. In the course of time Cain brought some of the fruits of the soil as an offering to the Lord. But Abel brought fat portions from some of the firstborn of his flock. The Lord looked with favour on Abel and his offering but on Cain and his offering He did not look with favour. So Cain was very angry and his face was downcast. Then the Lord said to Cain, 'Why are you angry? Why is your face downcast? If you do what is right will you not be accepted? But if you do not do what is right, sin is crouching at your door, it desires to have you, but you must master it.' Now Cain said to his brother Abel, 'Let's go out to the field,' and while they were in the field Cain attacked his brother Abel and killed him. Then the Lord said to Cain, 'Where is your brother Abel?' 'I don't know,' he replied, 'Am I my brothers keeper?' The Lord said, 'What have you done? Listen! Your brother's blood cries out to me from the ground. Now you are under a curse and driven from the ground, which opened its mouth to receive your brother's blood from your hand. When you work the ground it will no longer yield its crops for you. You will be a restless wanderer on the earth.' Cain said to the Lord, 'My punishment is more than I can bear. Today you are driving me from the land and I will be hidden from your presence. I will be a restless wanderer on the earth and whoever finds me will kill me.' But the Lord said to him, 'Not so, if anyone kills Cain he will suffer vengeance seven times over.' Then the Lord put a mark on Cain so that no one who found him would kill him.

Then verses 19-22:

Lamech married two women, one named Adah and the other Zillah. Adah gave birth to Jabel, he was the father of those who live in tents and raise livestock. His brother's name was Jubal, he was the father of all who play the harp and flute. Zillah also had a son, Tubal-Cain, who forged all kinds of tools out of bronze and iron. Tubal-Cain's sister was Naamah.

And then the final verse of the chapter,
"At that time men began to call on the name of the Lord." The New Living Translation says, "At that time men first began to worship God."

Let's paraphrase the chapter a little and look at some of the lessons that it contains.

When it came to harvest time, Cain, a farmer, brought God a gift from his farm produce. It was probably grain, fruits and vegetables. Abel, the shepherd, brought some choice lambs from his flock. Many commentators have assumed that the writer's description of the lambs that Abel brought as 'choice' and the absence of the word 'choice' in respect to the offering that Cain brought, implies that Cain's produce offering was probably of poorer quality. Now, for sure, the implication is fairly clear that Cain's gift is not as good as Abel's, but for the purpose of our reading of the passage let us not make that specific assumption.

The problem with focusing on that perception of the relative quality of the two offerings is that the worth or value of the gifts, in themselves, suddenly become the entire issue in their acceptability. I think that commentators have latched on to this explanation to try to understand what appears to be a measure of injustice on God's part. Two offerings, two different types of offering, but one rejected and one accepted. This would seem unfair, unless there is a definite reason for the refusal. Well, maybe one isn't quite as good as the other! That must be it! (Some other commentators feel that Cain took for granted that his offering should have been more acceptable since he was the firstborn child. This, I believe, is closer to the core truth of the passage.)

I want to suggest to you that the quality of Cain's gift is not the issue here. Rather, it is the motivation behind the gift that is the real problem. The gift is just a reflection of that motivation. At this stage, let us just agree that something was lacking in Cain's offering that made it unacceptable to God.

If we read on, we find there is something that God knows about Cain which directly affects that acceptability. The truth is that God knows Cain's heart. And because his heart is not right, his offering of worship is not acceptable. The quality of the gift reflected Cain's heart attitude. The inherent quality of the gift in itself is only part of the story, it was the heart behind the gift that was important.

Cain was angry that his offering was not accepted. "Why are you so angry?" asks God. "You, [your offering], will be accepted if you respond in the right way. But watch out, sin is waiting to attack and destroy you and you must subdue it." (NLT paraphrased)

God asks him to respond in the right way. If the offering in and of itself was inadequate, God would have made that abundantly clear. But God was looking beyond the physical presented offering for a heart reaction from Cain. He gave Cain another chance to rectify his mistake.

Cain, still enraged by what has happened and missing the opportunity entirely, takes his anger out on his brother Abel, eventually tricking his brother and killing him. He then denies all knowledge of the crime before God and in the fulness of time is eventually banished from the land.

The first thing that the story tells us is that these two brothers understood that they were required to make an offering to God. This story predates the giving of the Law to Moses, so this means that both Cain and Abel and their parents were entirely aware that bringing an offering to God was an essential part of relating to Him. An offering, of course, is essentially what worship and the heart of worship is all about. Whatever we do physically in our act of worship, it's all about bringing an offering to the Father.

So the first interaction between God and man after the Fall was to do with worship and, even more, with the heart of worship in man. That really is an indication, right away, of how important God feels worship is.

I've been to conferences where people have had seminars cutely titled, Worship Wars. I know there are at least two books using the same phrase in the title and that 'worship wars' has turned up in other books and Christian literature more than a few times.

I have already mentioned this but I think that is a really shameful title and an unfortunate choice of words. I feel quite strongly about it actually, because, as I hope you've seen in our first chapters, there were and are, indeed, worship wars taking place. But these are not pointless skirmishes in a church building somewhere, between traditional hymn factions and modern worship pioneers! These aren't the petty disagreements between the classical liturgist and the free-thinking postmodernist. Not at all.

The worship wars truly taking place are occurring, still, in the heavenly places themselves. War between the angels of Satan and his desire to be the one who is worshipped by men and women, against all of those whose desire is to see Jesus lifted high and the Father glorified. These are the real worship wars!

Spending so much time discussing the divisions and arguments that have sprung up over the style and type of songs that we sing during what's deemed the 'worship' on a Sunday seems quite pointless, does it not? It's almost like we're wasting time with intellectual argument about what is worship and what is appropriate worship and what is good worship and what is bad worship and most of the time doing a kind of Woman of Samaria thing. Jesus had already settled that argument some time ago.

The background to this story in the Bible, told in John 4, is that the Samaritans had disagreements with the Jews over heritage, race, the correct location of the Temple for worship and the books appropriate to Holy Scripture. In other words, they expressed doctrinal and historical differences from each other. (Sound familiar?)

Jesus met the woman at a well where she had come to draw water and He had paused in the heat of the day to get drink. In the course of their interaction, Jesus begins to engage her in conversation and asks some pretty direct questions about her life. In a response by the Samaritan woman, probably designed to deflect Christ from His unfolding of her less than perfect lifestyle, she asks a question of Jesus. (I've a friend who does that, always answers a question with a question. It's very annoying, right?) Her question is this: "Our fathers worshipped on this mountain, but you Jews claim that the place where we must worship is in Jerusalem." She was asking, "Who is right?"

Jesus' reply, of course, is that it doesn't really matter where you worship, so long as you worship in spirit and truth. You must worship in spirit and truth.

So, returning to Cain and his unacceptable offering, you have to ask yourself the question: "What is more important, the gift or the heart behind the gift?" And the answer, it has to be the heart. It cannot be the gift itself. Of itself it cannot just be the gift for about four reasons.

Number one, what would have happened if Cain had had a bad harvest?

As every farmer knows, a bad harvest will come around once in a while. You plant all the right seed at the right time, you try to anticipate the vagaries of the weather and the seasons but unfortunately, due to perhaps too much or too little rain, a bad harvest comes. In your offering you bring the best that you've got from that harvest, but maybe it isn't quite as good as a harvest taken up somewhere else where the weather was kinder.

Would God have rejected the offering that you bring? The firstfruits of a poor harvest? No, not at all. That would not have been fair.

God in His immeasurable mercy could not have said, "That gift's not very good, I don't want it." The fact is that God's acceptance or rejection of a worship offering has little or nothing to do with the intrinsic worth of the gift at all, it has to do with the heart behind that gift.

Another reason why the style, form and content of the offering are not, in themselves, important, is that the rest of the Bible doesn't support this. In the New Testament in Luke 21, Jesus is at the Temple. He witnesses a woman coming and making an offering of a virtually worthless coin called a widow's mite, the smallest denomination of coin in circulation at that time. Still, she gave it as her offering. Those that were rich and wealthy and had placed vast sums of money on to the offering would have regarded the mite as a meagre, very poor offering indeed, but not Jesus.

He saw it and He understood that out of her poverty what she was giving was everything. Out of her poverty she was expressing her love to God by giving everything she had. The gift in itself was as nothing, really, in the currency of that day, but the heart behind it was everything. Its value was measured not of itself, but in the context of the one who was giving it.

The third point about the gift that was brought by Cain is this, if the acceptability comes down to the gift and the quality of the gift only, then by implication, this suggests that God is hard to please.

In other words, we have to be careful that we don't get the impression that acceptable worship can only be given by the best crafted and most beautifully sung aria, and not by the tuneless rendition of a children's chorus by the nursery class in *crèche* on a Sunday. That can't be right. The Bible says that "out of the mouths of babes, God ordains perfect praise." The fact is, as hard as it may be to believe, because of the mystery of grace, our God is not 'hard to please'. We will never really please Him with what we think are quality gifts and talents. Whatever the gift looks or sounds like, God is always looking deeper.

Reading Revelation 5 amuses me a little when we get to the portion where John describes the angels of heaven numbering 10,000 times 10,000 singing with a loud voice! That's 100 million angels all singing together in perfect harmony. And, they're singing loudly. In comparison to the melody, force, volume and celestial harmony of that choir, even our best endeavours must pale into insignificance. And yet, despite this, it is as if sometimes God quiets the company of heaven itself and inclines an ear to the tuneless, simplistic song of some rural church choir in a rundown church building, small in number and weak in power, but as sweet to His heart and ear as the millions of angels that surround His throne. Why would that be? Simply because, whatever the sound, what will please Him most are broken and contrite hearts presented to Him in transparency and humility.

I am a big fan of the author and pastor Erwin McManus and he sometimes recounts a little thought process which I find very inspiring. It goes something like this:

"Isn't God really tough? Those Ten Commandments, come on, I mean, what do you expect? How could God ever expect us to meet and keep to such a high and lofty moral challenge as these?

Let's look at them. For example, don't lie, don't want things you can't have, don't kill people, be faithful to your partner, be nice to your mum and dad and have a rest once a week. It's ridiculous!"

Do you get what he's saying? The fact is, they're not really that hard at all. They are all pretty straightforward. Yet still we couldn't do it. God is, really, not that hard to please.

And, of course, this is all intrinsically linked to what Jesus did. Even though our God is most holy, high, lifted up and full of inexpressible and unfathomable glory, His Son Jesus, by His amazing sacrifice to His Father, made it possible for us to bring the little that we have, the poor widow's mite that we possess, and with our whole heart make it an offering that actually pleases God. Doing what pleases God, doing what is right, as God requests.

Sometimes the offering that we do bring might even fall short of our best intentions, might not be as accomplished or as great as we had intended, yet the perspective of a loving Father God will always be different

I do conferences these days on worship. I find myself in different climates and parts of the world entirely different from my hometown. One recent conference I completed was held in a part of the world with very low humidity levels in the climate. The air was dry and harsh.

Now those of you who use your voices a lot in speaking or singing will know that lack of moisture in the air, and equivalently down your throat, can wreak havoc with your vocal chords! You need to drink copious amounts of water and keep close to the nearest wash/rest room (for obvious reasons).

Well, I had been really busy. I had a bunch of seminars and worship sessions to do and I was having a great, if fairly busy, time. I never stopped talking and I didn't pay any attention to either the climate or my wasted throat. I missed coffees and down time and forgot to drink water and, generally, was totally irresponsible. People came up after different components of the events to ask questions and keep you talking some more. You feel like a real jerk if you excuse yourself and refuse to talk and so, you keep on babbling away there.

Still, I made it through hour after hour of session and when I finished my last worship set towards the end of the event, I thought, contentedly, "That's it!"

Not so! There was a major concert event that evening and due to some flight problems the headline band for the event couldn't make it until very late in the evening. My host asked if I would mind bouncing in a short 30 minute session at the start of the evening event to cover some empty space. Who could resist? The fact that there were to be 10,000 concert goers at the event in no way swayed my decision. Ah, the fickle fire of fame ignites once more!

Most of my band and musicians couldn't stay on as they had flights and buses to catch, but, undeterred, I managed to cobble together a small crew of acoustic musicians and singers and began to plan my new last event. We lost keyboards, drums, electric bass and guitar and were left with the bare bones of what was a little like some sort of 1960s type folk group. Despite all that was happening I thought, "Well, all we can ever do is to worship you, God." It might not sound too good but at least we'll worship with all our heart.

But first, I needed to do some shopping! The first rule of family life for a travelling worship leader (actually, it's the second rule – the first rule is don't travel that often) is make sure you have a gift for each of your little offspring when you get home. Offspring like presents! And so, a very kind volunteer drove me to a shopping centre.

Trouble was, they wanted to talk. They talked and conversed the whole way there and back in the car, and all the way around the stores as well. Again, what sort of self-centred jerk would have said, "I'm sorry, I cannot speak, for I am endeavouring to protect my voice." Probably me. But I chose not to and warbled on.

That evening 10,000 faces looked to the stage as the last minute stand-in special addition to the event was announced.

We charged straight into our set and interacted with the crowd and generally made as good a job of it as we could when suddenly on reaching for a particularly forceful and high note in one of my songs, I realised that all was not well.

I lost my voice. Totally and entirely. Couldn't sing, speak, or anything. Halfway through a song. Disaster! And only 10,000 people there to see it. Ah, fickle fire of fame, how easily thou art extinguished!

I whispered (loudly) to one of the backing vocalists that they would have to finish the set for me and they graciously did so. I stood with my guitar and played out the remaining songs. As that great social commentator Dick Dastardly would have said, "Drat and double drat!" It was a somewhat ropey performance.

I am pretty sure the rest of the event went without a hitch for the other bands and the latecomers and that no one else managed to lose their voice. But here's the funny thing. The organiser and host sent me an email a few weeks after the event. Of all the responses back from the folks that were at the concert night, the highlight for most was that wee band thing where the guy leading lost his voice. That's the bit that touched them.

There may be a number of reasons why that is the case. Perhaps it was just the oddity of the group, the unusual context and the voice losing thing. Maybe that is what made it memorable. But, in the midst of all of this, it might just be the fact that, no matter what we possess or have at our disposal at any time, God can take the least of all these, and through worship, do the greatest thing.

CHAPTER 7

Worship:
The Pursuit of God [2]

Back in Genesis 4 there is another point we can look at ...

God had begun a pursuit for Cain's worshipping heart, but it didn't end at the time when God told him his gift wasn't right. Even though, Cain did not respond in any way appropriately to what God had asked him to do.

We're pretty tough on Cain.

I met someone once on a Sunday in my church. He was a visitor and his name was Cain. Someone reading this book is likely to be called Cain also. But the name Cain, (not in your case, of course), has become synonymous with treachery and double-dealing and faithlessness. Abel is forever known as the good guy of the story and Cain is the bad guy. That's the way we understand it and, to be honest, it is true.

The trouble is, the thing about Cain is that all his stuff is our stuff. All the bad feeling, the jealousy, the anger at God, the rivalry and the bitterness, especially in the area of creative worship. Is that not true, or is it just me? Cain's heart is wrong, he brings his offering which, because of his heart, is not accepted. Does he fix it when God asks him to? No. He actually turns in a jealous rage upon his brother and goes so far as to murder him and try to cover up the evidence. It's all there in the early verses of the chapter.

Do you know that feeling you get when a close friend writes a song, or performs in an event, or produces a work of art and it's in the field that you want to excel in? Suddenly the song gets picked up, or the event is given glowing reviews, or perhaps that is the artwork which is sold at auction for a vast sum of money.

And what do you think?

Well, let's hope you're happy for them, but perhaps you're thinking, "Now, why did that happen? How did that happen? My song, my part, my painting was just as good, if not better. What's the deal here?"

I have a great friend in the USA called Paul Mills. He's one of the finest producers of music that I know. He has a great heart and is an incredibly humble guy. As a result of all the many projects he has been involved in over his long and illustrious career he has been recognised by the Gospel Music Association and awarded several Dove awards. A Dove is a little gold coloured statuette equivalent in his field to an Emmy, or a Grammy, or a Brit Award, or whatever. It is a tremendous accolade. I don't have one. (But I'm not bitter.)

He uses one as a door stop. A door stop! (Well, they are very heavy.) I was in his recording studio a few years back and as I opened the door I tripped on this beautiful piece of gold polished cast iron or whatever.

I said, "Oh! Sorry!"

And he said, "Whoops, just a moment," and shoved the award with the side of his foot up against the door to keep it open. That's humility. If I had one of those awards it would be sitting right there on a table beside my front door, so that people wouldn't miss it when they came to visit. "What's that?" "Oh, it's nothing, just my Dove award."

All Cain's stuff is our stuff. The jealousy of other people's accomplishments; getting angry, moping off when we don't succeed or achieve the instant success and recognition that we think we deserve. Everybody does it, from the greatest to the least. That 'old man' thought process that says, "Well, thanks a lot, I gave myself totally and look what happened. Thanks for nothing! I'm out of here, I've had enough, I did my best."

There it is. The wrong response to God's call, just like Cain. Yet, here's the thing about God's unsurpassable patience and grace, even when Cain fails to respond. When Cain commits a terrible crime filled with anger and jealousy, God should abandon him, but He doesn't.

The chronology of this passage really bugged me for a while because the preceding chapter (Genesis 3) tells the story of how man is driven away from the Garden of Eden after the Fall and sent "out from Gods presence." Then, in chapter four, when God gets to the stage where He has to chastise Cain for his wicked act, the Bible uses the same phrase, "Cain went out from the Lord's presence." At first reading I initially thought, "Oh no, there's one of those nasty little contradictions, that some of those really smart theologians will use to say that the Bible is contradicting itself. First, God sends Adam and Eve out from His presence and then, even though Cain is born outside the Garden, outside of God's presence, he is somehow sent out of God's presence again. How can that be correct?"

It's simple really.

Man, Adam and Eve, are put out of the Garden of Eden, put out of God's presence and fellowship because of their disobedience, and what happens?

God immediately goes after them. Man is put out of paradise and almost immediately a loving God steps out of paradise into the realm of man to pursue him.

It's the pursuing heart of God.

This is what the God who sent His Son, slain from before the foundation of the world, initiated as soon as the Fall of man occurred. From that very moment, the moment we forfeited paradise, God has been seeking to bring us back. That's why Christ said He had come to seek and to save those that were lost. This is our God, the God who pursues the lost. When God says to His wayward Cain, "You'll be a restless wanderer through the earth", He was reminding all of us of our state and position on this earth.

Even in the midst of his dreadful sin and actions, God did not break relationship with Cain. God would have been entirely just if He had simply pronounced judgment on Cain and sent him away. But, He talked to him, He reasoned with a murderer and He pursued him. That sounds wrong, doesn't it, but it actually looks like God didn't even condemn Cain.

If you look at the section where God confronts Cain, He says, "What have you done? Look what you've done, now you're under a curse."

It's almost as if God said, "Look at the consequences of what you have done."

The judgment came in the Garden of Eden when man fell. All the consequences of the choice that was made there, driven and motivated by the one who sought to be worshipped rather than to worship, are now active in our lives. The judgment had already been exacted, the damage already done. Cain's actions had a consequence because of the punishment he was already under.

So what God is telling Cain is this: the consequence of what you've done is that you're now under a curse because of your actions. The apostle Paul may be saying something like this in Romans 5:16 when he tells us that, "The judgment followed one sin and brought condemnation."

You can almost sense the despair in God's words. He's telling Cain the consequences of his action; Cain's foolishness and recklessness exacted the punishment on himself.

And yet there's one final stage in this incredible interaction between the wicked son and the Heavenly Father.

Cain gives a wrong or inappropriate offering in worship and is angered at God's refusal to accept it. God looks for him, seeks him out, meets with him, and says, "Get it right, Cain, fix it, give me your heart." But Cain ignores God's request and in a jealous rage murders his brother. God comes after him once again! God tells Cain the consequences of his actions with hardly a hint of exacting punishment or judgment on him. And then Cain has the audacity to say that the punishment is too great for him to bear and essentially asks for clemency. At this point you or I would be thinking, "Son, that's enough" and dispense with the boy right there and then.

But, amazingly, this is not what happens.

Cain is worried that, because of his reputation, if people see him they'll kill him because of what he has done.

I would have responded to this by saying, "Well – tough!"

Something like that.

But God, in another show of heavenly compassion, says "Not so" and puts a mark on him for his protection. There are some alternative translations to the phrase "not so" in different versions of the Bible. One is that God said, "Very well." If you want a modern equivalent of 'Very well' it's a bit like 'Okay'. What incredible mercy and unfathomable grace. Why is God doing this? What is God doing and what makes Him act like this?

The answer I believe is where the story started at the beginning of the chapter. God is after Cain's heart of worship. He's after our worship. The story started with an act of worship that was flawed and God is pursuing him to get him back into relationship, to get him back into that communication with his Father which is face to face before the throne of God in worship and love.

I'm sure you've been to a wedding at some time. I am fairly privileged in our church because when I attend a wedding it's often because I am playing music at the front and get to see, close up, the vows and exchanging of rings etc. I played at one not so long ago involving one of our members called Elaine.

When it came to the time for the vows to be said the couple turned to face each other.

Every time Elaine had to say a line of her vows, a big smile came across her face. It was the funniest thing to watch, because her smile was so radiant and big and full that she could hardly say the words!

Sorry, Elaine. It was just fantastic.

And I thought, you know what's going on here? This is like an act of worship. She could hardly get the words out because of the smile on her face. This is what God is after. He's after the heart, and the singers, and the worshippers and the painters and the dancers that can hardly get the action out because of the joy that is filling their souls.

He's so keen to get it, it seems there is a hint of divine flexibility. Now, I'll probably get into trouble for that, but that is what God seems to have done in this story. There is a consequence for our actions as the restless wanderers of the earth. But that right and just consequence can be set aside because of His mercy.

There's another point to be made about worship in this passage, before we get to the end of the chapter. And it's this, worship transcends all our lives.

In the middle of the chapter, verses 20-22 seem to be dropped in from nowhere in particular and mention three more offspring in the unfolding generations of men. But if we accept that the bulk of this passage has to do with worship, then there's something that we can learn from these few verses. One child was named Jubal, and the Bible says he was the father of all who played the harp. The other was called Jabal and he raised livestock. The last of the triplet was named Tubal-Cain and he made things.

There you have almost a little summary of practically all the actions of all the working men and women of the world in a nutshell – artisans, producers and builders.

We're looking here at all the great creative works that man can do. Farmers, supermarket workers, gardeners, contractors, house builders, shop assistants, musicians and artists, engineers and craftsmen.

(I noticed that lawyers and accountants are not in that list, you know, but I'm sure this is alright.)

What are these verses saying to us?

I believe it is saying something that we already know, but that is very, very important. It is telling us that every area of our lives can be worship.

Every one, no matter what you do, no matter what your gift is, every area of life from the greatest musician or greatest artist to the simple labourer or person who can't find a job – from the home maker to the house builder, from the hands that fashion clay to the head that fathoms complex athematics. Everything you do can be an act of worship. Everyone is a worshipper.

I was born and still live in Northern Ireland. You've probably heard someone use the phrase, the 'Protestant work ethic'. Well, Northern Ireland is pretty much where that phrase was born.

If you stand on the roof of my church in Belfast and look to the northwest you can see two massive cranes which are located in the shipyard, we call them Samson and Goliath. Once these were the largest cranes in the world. This is the shipyard where they built the ocean-going liner, Titanic. In World War 2, Belfast made more ships for the war effort than any other shipyard in Europe.

It was and still is a massive industrial heartland in the city and there's something in the Belfast person, (of all religious persuasions) that still holds this 'work ethic'. In 1900, 75% of the population of Belfast were immigrant workers come to the city to find jobs. It is a city built on working men and women of all faiths, creeds and backgrounds. They came to do a good job and to do it well. There is something in our psyche that is constantly trying to be excellent.

And, of course, many of you reading this will also hold to this ambition. You want to do the job well. You want to pursue excellence. And it is absolutely okay to pursue excellence in what you do, in fact it's important for us, so long as you remember one thing.

Never let the pursuit of excellence be the pursuit of your heart.

In fact, the apostle Paul reflects on this issue beautifully in 1 Corinthians 13 when he says:

I will show you still a more excellent way. If I speak in the tongues of men and of angels, but have not love, I am only a resounding gong or a clanging cymbal. If I have the gift of prophecy and can fathom all mysteries and all knowledge, and if I have a faith that can move mountains, but have not love, I am nothing. If I give all I possess to the poor and surrender my body to the flames, but have not love, I gain nothing.

He talked about love, about that relationship, that love affair with God which is, in effect, the basis for our worship.

So all the things that we do, everything that we find that God has gifted us in, all these things can and should be acts of worship. The action itself is not the worship; it is an act that, hopefully, expresses the heart of our worship. And so we endeavour to make sure that, in the middle of it all, if we pursue excellence, we pursue it only because of our love for the Lord.

Don't fall into Cain's trap.

If you think about it, Abel's offering would have been worthless as well if it had not been carried along with a heart that wanted to bring the best to God. Just bringing the best that we have, following an instruction or a tradition, can be as worthless an act of worship as Cain's. It is the heart behind the gift.

I know some theologians will remind us that the event is also to be seen as a picture of the ultimate sacrifice of Christ and compares the bloodless offerings of Cain with the sacrificial acts of Abel. But God does take time throughout the Scriptures to tell us that He has no desire for the offering of sacrifice unless the offering is presented by a humble and contrite heart (cf. Isaiah 1:11).

Let me ask you three questions as we near the end of this section. These are my three favourite questions on this area and they are designed to reveal the desires of your heart. We will return to them later on in the book, but for now…

Ask yourself these:

1. If the only person to hear my songs, to hear my sermons, to hear my talks, to see me dance, to look at my paintings, whatever, if that only person was God, would that be sufficient? If no one else heard the songs that you write, would it be entirely sufficient that you were able to sing them to God?

2. Can God really open doors that no man can shut? (Well, of course, He can and He can also shut doors that no man can open. But do you accept this fact and can you live in the grace and goodness of it?) Do we all understand that what we give, we give to Him alone and what happens after that is nothing to do with us and all to do with Him?

3. Finally, have you ever said, "God has told me that my songs/ sermon/ writings/ artwork are very important and it is essential that I get maximum exposure because the Church really, really needs to see and hear my stuff!"

The correct answers to these three questions should be, Yes, Yes, and No in that order!

Watch out for that last one, by the way. The wrong answer to that question reveals a great deal about your heart. The old Baptist theologian, F B Meyer, once said that "there was no room for ambition in the Church." I'd like to modify this wise statement by saying that there is absolutely no room for selfish ambition in worship.

Better the heart that says, "God, you pursued me to capture me in order that I might be your worshipper and worship you alone. If other people like these songs, if other people like my paintings, if other people like the way I dance, if any of that encourages other people to worship, well, that's great, but it is not the most important thing. In fact, it's not even anything." If you can say all this in truth, then you have the heart of a worshipper.

Let me tell you quickly about the album, Revival in Belfast. If you're reading this book you may either have a copy of the album or you've heard about it. But, if not, in short, the release of the Praise and Worship CD entitled Revival in Belfast by Integrity Music not only established the songs of worship from my home church on the international level, but also increased the profile of the church itself and, possibly, the Christian witness in Northern Ireland to a world stage. My church, Christian Fellowship Church or CFC, had evolved from a small group of Christian students who back in the late 1970s and early 80s devoted themselves to praying for Northern Ireland and the troubled circumstances in which we found ourselves.

In 1987, after a number of stages in growth from those small but committed beginnings, Paul Reid was asked to assume the leadership of the church that had been established. Along with the elders he selected a tenfold statement of beliefs or aspirations for the church, the first of which was a devotion to Praise and Worship. Praise and Worship was to be the principal cornerstone of this growing church. I joined no more than a month after Paul moved into fulltime ministry and, in the fulness of time, the songs that were written in CFC were formed and fuelled by the experiences of the church and the environment that we were part of. Our desire was to glorify God the Father, Son and Holy Spirit, and the songs that flowed from this purpose were nothing more or less than the fruit of those desires.

People will always ask, "How did that album happen, what did you do to cause it to have such an influence in Christian worship music? How did you do it?"

The truth of the matter is that fundamentally it all comes down to one member of my church fellowship, Ronnie Irvine. Ronnie loves music and was a radio DJ for some time, but he is not in the worship teams in CFC. He is not involved in any of the 'arty' type ministries in the church at all but, rather, he serves voluntarily in a missionary organisation. Ronnie owned and managed a shoe store on the east side of Belfast for many years. An excellent business-man, his other passion was for missions, and much of his spare time and finance was put to that purpose.

On nearing retirement from the business, he became the Northern Ireland representative for Haggai Institute Ministries, a worthy missionary organisation dedicated to the training and sending of indigenous missionaries to the countries in which they were born and live. Every year or so they have conferences for their supporters and sponsors in different parts of the world.

A few years back Ronnie happened to be in North America and met a guy called Steve from Integrity Music, one of the record companies in the USA. Steve was along at the conference as a delegate as well. They got to talking, as you do, and once they had established what each did for a living and where they came from,

Steve said, "We'd like to come to Belfast, there must be some interesting styles of worship in Ireland."

Ronnie replied, "Well, why don't you come to our church, because it's really great."

That was about it, really.

In the course of six or seven months, this 'chance' meeting led to a visit to Belfast by Steve Merkel from Integrity, followed by a series of discussions and relationship building but eventually the church hosted a night of worship, recorded by Integrity, and the album was produced.

We had no ambitions for the recording, we had no idea what would happen to it, to be honest we didn't really mind one way or another; our primary concern was just to have a great night of worship music. But, of course, God had other plans. He took what was done on that night and used it for His purposes all over the world.

The thing is, of course, neither that night, the recording, or the ensuing 'success' (if I might use that word on this occasion) would never have happened, if one of our members who is interested in missions had not just been in a certain place at a certain time and in a short conversation invited someone to come to our church.

God opens doors that no man can shut and uses people that you wouldn't even regard as part of the 'worship team'. Everyone is a potential worshipper and God is in pursuit of their worshipping heart, no matter what they do or who they are.

It's good to remember this when you're picking your worship groups or choir members or other creative teams. A few years ago in CFC the then Worship Pastor, Gary Mills, decided to put together a worship prayer team that didn't have any of the actual worship team leaders in it. They were to meet regularly and bring prayers and supplications for the whole area of creative worship in the church before God.

I was one of those leading worship at the time and I just couldn't get my head round his decision not to include the worship teams. I kept thinking, "Surely the worship leaders at least should be in that prayer team." But once you understand that everybody is a worshipper and not just the folks that play instruments or sing, then it all makes perfect sense. Just because you play a guitar or paint a picture doesn't make you any more important when we're worshipping at the throne of God.

The reality is that we have all of our lives, all of our ambitions and hopes, all of the things that take up our work time, our family time and our recreational time. We do all this with our hearts filled with worship.

I said this was the final point, but there is one last message for worshippers in the closing phrase of the chapter (verse 26). I think the best translation is in the New Living Bible, and it says this,

"… people first began to worship the Lord."

A boy called Enosh is born and in his lifetime, men "begin to worship the Lord." Now, this is interesting; the Bible, of course, was not originally structured in chapters, with punctuation and sections and all the cross references that we've become used to. The chapters didn't get incorporated until the 15th century or thereabouts. But this verse establishes a definite end to a section of narrative. Chapter 5 presents the genealogy from Adam to Noah and chapter 6 moves on to a written account of Noah's life.

The last verse of chapter 4 concludes the story of the Creation and the Fall and the start of God's pursuit of man. It finishes with the words that in Enosh's time people first began to worship the Lord. Enosh can be translated as 'Mankind'. Is God letting us know that the desire of His heart is for the worship of all mankind, and that He will, in the fulness of days, obtain it when every knee shall bow and every tongue confess that Jesus is Lord?

If I could be so bold as to paraphrase all of what chapter 4 is saying, I believe that God's word to us is this,

"Listen. You were made for worship, I desire your worship, but one who also desires worship stole your heart. I want that worshipping heart back. You are mine and I want your worship. I will do anything to get your worship, I will do anything to draw your heart to me. I will be gracious in how I deal with you. I will go and do the most extreme thing possible to bring you back to paradise, to capture your heart. I will take and honour worship from whatever you do, wherever you are, if your heart's for me."

And, at the end of this chapter, God gets that worship that He has been pursuing.

Mankind begins to worship the Lord.

Is this a picture of the continuing pursuit of God for the worshipping hearts of men? Do these early chapters in Genesis reflect the purpose of God's plan of salvation for you and me? Was not the sacrificial action of Jesus Christ the most spectacular act of worship that could have been presented? And has He not, by that sacrifice, made it possible for us to worship His Father again, just as it was in paradise? I believe that this is the case.

We don't know if Cain ever made it, of course. We do not know if he finally responded and began to worship God. That's the sad part of the story. According to 1st John, the writer says that Cain "belonged to the evil one and was always doing what was evil." So the indication there is that Cain never actually made it; he never figured it out. Despite the lengths that God went to in order to rescue Cain and reconcile him to Himself, Cain, unfortunately, did not respond. Perhaps one reason why God is angry when people don't give Him the worship He deserves and why there are such dreadful consequences for peoples and nations, is because of the lengths that He went to in order to win that worship back.

And still there's one more glorious truth in this pursuit of God. A little Emmaus Road experience.

He steps out of paradise to pursue us, and by the presence and power of His Holy Spirit we finally understand and accept the salvation that His Son Jesus has provided. We surrender to the pursuit and we begin to worship God. Then the One who pursued us, begins to pass by and we, then, become the pursuers! So, captivated by the beauty and grace and mercy of God that we, now, pursue Him in worship as He unfolds His purposes for our lives. He, ahead of us, running higher and faster with greater visions. We run, we start to pursue the One who pursued us. The pursuit of worship becomes our pursuit for God's heart.

CHAPTER 8

The View from the Sidelines

So far we have established how important worship is and that everything and everyone, including you and me, were created to worship. We have shown that, amongst the many spiritual dynamics and motivations that were involved, the very Fall of man came down to an issue of worship.

We have further noted that God undertook a pursuit to get that worship back and we know that the One by which He has restored the relationship between Himself and men was His Son, Jesus Christ, as John 17 tells us Christ's desire and purpose was to bring glory to the Father. Verse 4 says, "I have brought you glory on earth by completing the work you gave me to do." Anglican Bishop Graham Cray describes Jesus as 'Heaven's Worship Leader' since His express purpose was to glorify the name of His Father.

We have further shown that worship misplaced has terrible and far reaching consequences for individuals, communities, and even nations, and that the Father's heart is to draw us back to worshipping Him, for His name's sake, and even because of His grace, for our sake.

We have shown, then, that how men worship, that is, the means that they use to express that worship, is pretty insignificant, really, in comparison to the attitude of the heart.

Well, if I'm right so far, then following the pattern of the history of Israel in the book of Kings that we reviewed, a few things would be likely to happen. And they would not be particularly good.

Imagine that you were some sort of a stocktaking angelic being standing at around the time of the resurrection of Jesus and, whilst all the other angels are going absolutely crazy with praise and worship to the risen Son of God, you, instead, are quietly reviewing all that is happening, past, present, and future. (Just doing your job!)

You might take a glance back through the history of God's chosen people and see how they continually abandoned the worship of God, or combined that worship with other so-called gods, or followed the practice but lost the heart. Or worse, cared little about what or who they worshipped. It wouldn't take you long to note these things. All the way through the books of Kings and Chronicles you can see it happening again and again.

You could also probably make a few wry predictions about the same thing happening in the Church as it grows. Perhaps over the years to come you would hazard a guess that some of the following circumstances might occur:

Occasionally, the Church will lose its focus in worship and the Father might have to re-ignite that passion again.

The Church will probably get around to idolising things and objects and maybe even other gods as opposed to the risen Lord.

There will probably be frequent arguments and disagreements on the form of worship, even though that has little importance, and people may even fall out over these disagreements.

At some time and in some places the form of worship will continue, but the heart and passion behind it will become cold.

Sound familiar?

As I previously said, one of the commonest questions I am asked, as, I'm sure, are practically every other worship leader, is this:

"What do you do when people disagree over what we sing in church?"

The main problem with this question is that it's the wrong question!

Maybe the best way to carry our worship journey forward is to share a few more things about myself and my personal experience and observations and see if you would agree.

My life began in a small terraced house in Spruce Street, in an area of Belfast, Northern Ireland called Donegall Pass. My father was a gentle, hardworking man employed for most of his life in the aircraft factory in Belfast. My mother was a feisty country girl who had moved to the city when she was a young teenager to take up a position as a maid and mother's helper with one of the more affluent families.

They were both God-fearing people, as folks were described in those days, and after their marriage attended one of the Presbyterian Churches in the area. We moved house when I was 2 years old to a property on the east of the city. In the 1960s, East Belfast was the industrial heart of the entire Province with tens of thousands of men and women employed in the shipbuilding, heavy machinery, aircraft and rope-making industries.

I, along with my older sister Jacqueline and younger brother Laurence, were baptised as infants into the Presbyterian Church in Ireland because of the lifelong membership of my parents.

The Presbyterian Church is pretty much the main Protestant denomination in Ireland and local history is writ large with respect to the influence of the members of this denomination, right across the spectrum of religious and political life. The earliest emigrants to the USA from Ireland, well before the tragic famine that forced a major emigration in 1845, included a large group of dissenting Presbyterians fleeing the oppression of the Anglican Church of those days.

Presbyterians formed the bulk of the United Irishmen of the 18th Century, seeking separation from their English masters and yet Presbyterians also formed the core of the Orange Order's formation in the same 18th Century, seeking to preserve a Protestant tradition from the influence of the stronger Catholic Church in the south of the island. When Northern Ireland separated from the South in 1921, Presbyterians were the major denomination represented amongst those who formed the new state of Northern Ireland, part of the United Kingdom, separate from the larger Republic of Ireland, or 'Free State' in the south.

Northern Ireland has always been a small country. It measures some 100 miles broad and deep and, consequently, had little apparent significance in world affairs before the 1970s when 'The Troubles' began.

Ireland as a whole is not that big either. Around 5.5 million people live on an island on the western tip of Europe which could still fit several times over into the state of Texas.

That's not to say Irish men and women don't influence world events; millions of residents of the USA, Canada, Africa, Australia and New Zealand can trace their ancestry back to Irish roots. Many world leaders, political reformists, artists, literary luminaries and business entrepreneurs were either born in Ireland, north and south, or are children of Irish stock. Indeed, a generally held belief is that a large part of the evangelism of Europe and much of the world throughout the past two millennia, has been fuelled and powered by Irish Christians.

However, it's also probably fair to say that, irrespective of what impact our troubled recent past and our famed ancient history has had, in the late 20th Century at least, much of what developed in the Christian Church in terms of reformed ideas on worship, and the change in worship music, happened independently and without any real influence of the Church in Ireland.

So there I was. A working class boy raised in a working class area along with my brother and sister by two good, hardworking parents.

It was standard procedure in those days, not that long ago, for any and all children from the Protestant culture to be sent to Sunday School, irrespective of their parent's level of conviction.

For probably no greater reason than the corresponding proximity to our house after we moved to the east (closer than the Presbyterians), I was, from the age of 3 or 4 raised a Congregationalist. I also spent Wednesday early evenings in the local Brethren Gospel Hall at their children's meetings until 10 years old, and then transferred to the church closest to our house in East Belfast. It was called Bloomfield Methodist and it was within walking distance of my home.

In 1969 what became known as 'The Troubles' began in Northern Ireland and in the early 1970s my teenage years were spent visiting and attending that little Methodist Church, a sanctuary from the harsh political and conflict-ridden society that we lived in.

People always want to ask, "What was it like growing up in the midst of the troubles in Northern Ireland?"

Well, by grace and God's protection, my brother, sister and I were fortunate to be spared from a great deal of the more wicked crimes that took place in our country. For sure we suffered discouragement, hopelessness and frustration at the incessant terrorist activities that stretched for almost 30 continuous years, but, at the time, it was a normal enough life. The truth is wherever you may have lived and grown up, be it good or bad, for you this becomes your normality. Many of my fellow countrymen and women, of course, were not so fortunate and over 3,000 people died with countless more thousands injured over that bleak period in our history.

At various times in those formative years in the Methodist Church at Bloomfield I was part of a fairly tough youth club, a member of a fairly not so tough Christian Endeavour youth meeting, and an assistant leader in the Youth Fellowship in the Manse on a Sunday night after church.

The only interest I had in music was that I enjoyed listening to it and for a couple of weeks when I was around 14 years old, like every other young man at some time or another, I wanted to be a rock star!

The reason I tell you all this, just in case you're totally bored at this point, is to inform you that when the latest worship revolution took place between the 70s and 80s, with the Graham Kendrick's and Chris Bowater's in the UK and the Don Moen's and Bob Fitts' in America, the position of the Church in Ireland was one, really, of an interested observer.

We watched the development of new songs and styles of worship from the sidelines.

There was little if any corresponding emergence of new worship hymn writers from Ireland in those early years. It's fair to say that in terms of the growth and development of new worship music styles in Ireland, the Church was around 10 years behind the UK and North America. Indeed, one of the sole sources of 'new worship' in Ireland were folks who many years ago formed the core of the church I presently belong to and who used the words of numerous Charles Wesley hymns, known and obscure, set to new melodies.

But it was a good place to be.

In those early days we were blessed by visits to Belfast by folks like Noel Richards, John Wimber, Trish Morgan, Larry Morgan, and other sturdy souls who braved the difficult political circumstances of the time to bring us their new songs of worship.

We were also in the enviable position of being able to sift, pick and choose the new stock of Christian music to find the songs, hymns and alternative worship styles that seemed most appropriate to our corporate and individual worship.

We could, therefore, receive the blessings of these new times without necessarily wading into the occasional conflicts that seemed to arise between traditionalists and reformists in the worship music genre. In a sense, it was possible to watch the development of new worship from the sidelines; close enough to have influence and be influenced by the changing times, but far enough away to have a better perspective of matters that unfolded.

It was, indeed, a good place to be!

And so I come to the main point of this chapter and something that I believe is important in the context of where worship is at present. If you like, it's a counter argument to what I believe is a peculiar mindset currently bubbling under the whole contemporary worship scene.

A number of recent texts have charted the perceived history of the recent upsurge in new worship and attempted to make some sort of chronological or historical sense of all that occurred. Most of the time the writers attribute the rise in new songs and expressions to the effects of other sociological phenomena, like the pop music era or other popular cultural expressions.

Occasionally they will attribute the events to the actions of one or more influential media personnel. If you want to read some of this perspective there are a few titles listed in the book list at the back of this book where you will encounter such thoughts.

The opinions expressed generally see commercial and cultural influences as shaping the new worship music 'scene' and refer to the simplicity and blandness of some of the new worship as a confirmation of this fairly negative opinion.

Whilst these are probably worthy enough perspectives, they certainly suffer, in my opinion, from what could be described as 'wood from the trees' syndrome.

By this I simply mean that incidents and circumstances viewed and perceived by those close to or immersed in the situations themselves often lack adequate perspective when attempting to analyse and explain the reasons for the developments that took place.

What might reasonably appear to the external observer as a clear sign of God's planning and handiwork, may seem to the hapless individual in the middle of all that happened as simply the result of men's actions and plans. This is often reflected in biblical stories like those of Gideon, Moses and Jeremiah, who in the midst of their circumstances and journeys would not have had any concept of the vast purposes that God had for their lives and often, even at nearing the end of those journeys, could only see the limitations and foolishness of their endeavours. But this is not necessarily a true reflection of the events that were occurring or which would come to pass.

In short, I don't believe what happened in contemporary worship was simply popular culture driven by, or the result of, the influence of ordinary people in influential jobs.

I'd like to proffer a different interpretation of what happened over the past 30 or 40 years in the Christian Church. Some of you may understand the next section in the context of what is called Restoration Theology.

The writer A P Gibbs named his tremendous book on worship, *Worship – the Christian's Highest Occupation*.

In the pages of this great work he endeavours to explain, based on Scripture, why he also believes that worship, in all its many-faceted expressions and variations, must be the highest calling of the believer. It's really impossible to summarise this book but, if I may, essentially what Gibbs says is as follows:

Above and beyond the saving action of Christ's sacrifice and our newly redeemed status, or the call on our lives in service, fantastic though these are, God's main desire is to draw a people close to Him that will truly worship. His desire is to be in that restored relationship of intimacy where the heart of man is fully given to God and he is fully in communion with Him. To fully know, and to be fully known. As it were, to be in such intimate relationship with the Father through the Son that we can walk and talk with Him in the cool of the evening and be so enraptured by who He is, what He has done and the incredible fact that the Almighty God of the universe wishes to commune with us continually, our hearts overflow with worship.

You've probably figured that I agree with the late great A P Gibbs on this!

The worshipping heart is the evidence and core of our right relationship with Him and that's what He desires.

And, of course, Gibbs is not alone in his assessment. A W Tozer's great message delivered in the 1960s near the end of his earthly ministry was that worship was the 'missing jewel in the evangelical church'. His testimony being that a right revelation of the majesty of God has but one effect, to draw unconditional worship from the believer. How timely that this message, now often remembered by commentators, preceded an explosion of new worship experience in our societies.

So, let me pose a question to you, which might initially seem a little sacrilegious, but ultimately, I hope, will move your thoughts to reconsider why this explosion of new worship has occurred at his time.

Here it is!

Imagine for a moment that you are God, (now stay with me here!).

It's the late-middle of the 20th Century. In earthly terms around the late 1960s, early 1970s. Once again, exasperatingly so to us, but not to the Father of all mercies, you have watched how the trappings of empty rituals, empty words and songs that had gone beyond the understanding of normal ordinary people had masked true worship. Meaningless activity has replaced heartfelt worship.

As has happened one hundred and two hundred years ago, and even a few thousand years previous to that, men had managed to place form and style and tradition over the response of the heart.

We had become like little Cain's, east of Eden, having the form but no substance of worship. The consequences of this, for us and our churches and the communities we live in, are disastrous.

Might you then not decide, as you have lovingly and graciously done before, to begin a process of restoration in the hearts of believers, fuelled and spurred by the Holy Spirit?

If worship, that fundamentally important factor of the believer's life, had somehow been moved in our understanding to being some sort of activity on one or two mornings each week in a 'place of worship' and your desire was to restore that worship lifestyle, might you not want to stir up your Church again in this realisation?

If the Church had lost the meaning and importance of worship, would you not, as a loving Heavenly Father, want to pursue a course of action to restore that place of importance?

I believe you might. For this whole scenario has happened before and God has moved before in much the same way.

And when He did, for some reason it was in the form of renewed musical praise.

Whether this praise reflected the work of the Holy Spirit in men's hearts and was a reaction to that work, or indeed was the actual work that the Holy Spirit initiated to give glory to the Father, I'm not sure. But it's enough to say that God has done it before!

When John Newton was moved to write songs of praise and worship to help the illiterate lace workers of his congregation understand the glory of God. When John and Charles Wesley determined to reach the lost and unlearned of Britain, who had become far removed from the established Church. When Isaac Watts began his non-conformist church in the heart of the London Docklands. When William Booth hammered out a song of victory over guilt, sin, addiction, poverty and cruelty on the Victorian backstreets.

Over the centuries God's hand has moved to restore the spirit and truth of worship to the Church using men and women with gifts that related to creative song writing. In their day they often suffered great humiliation and negativity from the intellectual elite. Watts was a versifier and not a proper poet! Booth was a shanty song singer, Wesley was an upstart pandering to the 'great unwashed'.

But no matter. God had shaken up their creative hearts to pen songs, not originally regarded for their high quality, but sung with renewed vigour by the newly converted hearts of the people. Worship was restored.

And so, being a gracious Heavenly Father, might you not begin in this particular generation of apparently great knowledge and worldly intellectual wisdom, almost as with a little child.

Might you, perhaps, introduce through the servant hearts of musicians and singers simple songs of one or two lines, with repetition and simplicity in the structure and melody, so that the hearts of your people could be drawn back to their Father again? So that people might learn to worship in intimacy once more?

Might not some of the songs be initially 'horizontal' in content, maybe clumsy and awkward and be more of encouraging each other, slowly developing into 'vertical' songs that give glory to God?

Might you not nurture and draw out of the mouths of babes and sucklings in the faith an increased and deepening understanding of what worship is?

And so, if this perspective is correct, then all the arguments in the world about song styles, traditional versus modern, instrumentation and why and who and how and all of that, are little more than a diversion. Rather than being a man-ordained phenomenon, is this renewed worship not more likely to be a God-ordained phenomenon?

Is it possible that God might have ordained the most recent wave of worship writing and creativity just to restore the heart of worship in His Church and that influential folk artists had absolutely nothing to do with it?

Is it possible that in the fight for the restoration of worship, the hearts of men, and the desire of all the nations that God would use not just warriors, but WARRIOR POETS? Those not known initially by their educational or theological background, not even of high musical training and poetic abilities. But hearts set on fire to worship God with everything at their disposal.

I truly believe that this is certainly a much more likely explanation of the history of what has happened recently in worship.

God is pursuing our worshipping hearts. Jesus says that He is seeking worshippers.

Some during this time were worried about 'throwing the baby out with the bathwater' by replacing some of the grand traditional hymns with what they perceived as second rate new ones, but there was little need to worry. Where the content and reference of the hymn was relevant, these have survived and contributed to our sung worship.

And those of us who struggle to remind people that our worship is not simply what we sing, but is lifestyle based, should take heart that the explosion of new songs of worship was paralleled by a new understanding of the need for a worshipping lifestyle in every area of our walk. I firmly believe if the renaissance of sung worship had not been of God, the accentuated understanding of worshipping lifestyles would not have followed.

How gracious our God is. The one truly sacrificial act of our lives, that of giving worship to Him, has been restored by Him to the Church with all the evidence of a nurturing Father at work.

What instruments has God used to bring this Renaissance about? Well, the same as He always has. Men and women. Ordinary servant hearts. Those not often regarded as 'special' in the eyes of the world, but those whom God has called.

WARRIOR POETS, called to fire up the worshipping hearts of the Church, that they might serve the God who pursued them by His mercy. Century after century, God calls ordinary men, women and children to stand in the gap for Him.

Who will He continue to use?

The WARRIOR POETS of this century, the 21st Century.

CHAPTER 9
Warrior Poets of the 21st Century

The next portion of this book is directed, I suppose, at those WARRIOR POETS, whoever they are and wherever they may be, that God is continuing to fire up. Those that will be inspired to find the place of worship and, with that unique expression that can only be theirs because of their history and culture and experience, touch the hearts of men and women all over the world. But, if you are one of the millions in the body whose gifts don't appear to be in the area of worship leading or song writing or other creative ministries, please don't stop reading.

I hope to show that the WARRIOR POETS are many and varied and often, in the eyes of the world, entirely inappropriate for the call God places on their lives. I also hope to show that, as is always the case, outside of the support and love and compassion of those in relationship with them, they are often unable to carry their mission very far.

There are many parts to the body of Christ, but not one part is more superior or necessary than another. Remember my friend Ronnie Irvine, erstwhile shoe salesman and missions supporter, and how he was instrumental in the advancing of worship music from our church? His right word in season has impacted the lives of millions of people all over the world.

Anointing and Choices – Who chooses the Warrior Poets?

Many of us either may aspire to, or perhaps are currently in post as, worship leaders in our fellowships and churches.

The rest of us have the pleasure, or otherwise, of being exposed to this ministry at least once a week! That this is a significant position to be in and one which carries great responsibility goes without saying.

But the thing is, whatever God's call is on our lives, have you ever wondered about the sequence of events that brought you to this place? And have you ever wondered how, at the end of it all, age, social status, looks, earthly location or environment matter little in God's economy? He seems to enjoy picking people for roles that, at first, seem entirely inappropriate. I often say that God seems to love choosing 'losers' to accompany His tasks.

Of course, He does.

1 Corinthians 1:25, "For the foolishness of God is wiser than man's wisdom, and the weakness of God is stronger than man's strength."

In the Old Testament, He chose Moses, (couldn't speak well), Jeremiah (too young), Gideon (hiding away from trouble), Joseph (arrogant and youthful) to further His plans for the human race. In the New Testament, Jesus picked tax collectors, fishermen, thugs, argumentative brothers and eventual traitors to be numbered among His closest friends.

It's almost like God goes out of His way to pick the unlikely to do the unbelievable.

He picked David the young shepherd boy, the youngest and overlooked son of his father Jesse and turned him into the sweet psalmist of Israel and a man after God's own heart.

You may recall the story in 1 Samuel 16. Samuel is instructed by God to go to Jesse's house and anoint the future King of Israel. After working through the eligible sons, Samuel insists on seeing David and on his entrance is instructed by God to anoint the boy with oil.

Here's the big question. At that point when Samuel anointed David, how many of the life choices made by David, by his father, and even by others in his family had preceded this apparent sudden discovery and decision?

How many songs had David sung over the sheep under his care on the lonely Israeli hillside? How many times had David struggled with adversity, coped with danger or made good decisions? Was he a naturally gifted musician, or did he pick up an elder brothers discarded harp one day and teach himself to play? Did he lie prone on the hillside over his family home and ponder deep thoughts as he surveyed the stars of heaven? Was he content to watch over the sheep? He certainly saw himself as a warrior, had he even contemplated a kingly role?

In other words, if you're waiting for the anointing as a Psalmist in God's kingdom now, or even if you're orchestrating your career and ambitions to make it possible, one thing must happen before you will ever have that responsibility.

God has to pick you.

I can remember the two occasions reasonably clearly, though the actual times and dates have become blurred as years have passed. They were two small but significant events where I made decisions which were to impact my entire life story.

It was definitely summer time and I was a young teenager living in East Belfast at the height of what has become known as 'The Troubles'. I was a nominal Christian, and no more. It wasn't till a few years later that I gave my life to Christ. My father had died shortly before this time as a result of lung cancer. I was 15 years old, he was 52 and the sweetest man I have ever known. One of his good friends, on reflecting on my dad's life said this, "For as long as I knew him, I never heard your father say a bad word against anyone." To say a bad word against anyone was Belfast-speak for criticism or a judgmental attitude. That this was true of the man and not just convenient platitudes uttered by a friend at a sad time, was never in doubt.

Somewhere in the great gene pool of life I suppose I inherited his gentle spirit. I was never an aggressive child, or adult, and preferred to keep what facial features I had well away from the fist or foot of any assailant that might have appeared. I think the proper word may be 'coward', but I'd rather not admit to that.

But even for a gentle soul, those were troubled days. Most of the history of those times and the propaganda that has accompanied the story recorded by all the countless numbers of journalists, commentators and historians, does little more than express someone's opinion or perspective. That's the deal. People will always write from some perspective and it's almost impossible to find a review of an event that is without bias.

So, please forgive me if what I am about to say doesn't sound correct or doesn't tally with what you've been told about our history. I can assure you it was, and is, truth to me.

The Provisional Irish Republican Army was one of the world's most ruthless and vicious terrorist factions. Through probably incredibly stupid political decisions and undoubted bigotry, the politics of Northern Ireland had given rise to a disaffected Nationalist population, mainly Catholic in religion, who perceived that in the area of jobs, homes, funding and status they were second-class citizens living in an unsustainable State. That this State, consisting of about 10,000 square miles and six 'counties', was owned and managed by the British Government when the larger part of Ireland was under its own authority and rule, added fuel to the fire. Even the police force was 90% Protestant due to a combination of factors.

Some peaceful Civil Rights marches in the Province, (mirroring some of the Black Civil Rights Marches in America), had resulted in riots and clashes between the Northern Irish Police (the RUC), and some Protestants who didn't care much for the marchers' rights.

The northeastern corner of Ireland is a large part of one of the four Irish provinces and is called Ulster. Over many hundreds, maybe thousands, of years until the 19th Century, it had shared emigration and immigration, not across the Atlantic Ocean, but across the short stretch of water known as the Irish Sea to Scotland. The heritage of this part of the island of Ireland became more of a mixture of Scots, Irish and a few other races.

By the 17th and 18th Century it had become a predominantly Presbyterian culture, whereas the remainder of Ireland had a more Catholic population. In the great Irish Revival of 1859, the vast majority of the 100,000 conversions that took place occurred in this part of the island.

In the early 1900s Ireland as a whole began to express through political and revolutionary methods a desire to be separate from

British rule. Britain and its Empire controlled and ruled over the island of Ireland. In the Northern corner the Ulstermen didn't agree with these aspirations and expressed a wish to stay within the United Kingdom.

To cut a very long and complex story short, in 1921 Ireland was partitioned into a 26 county 'Free State' to become known as the Republic of Ireland, whilst Northern Ireland remained part of the United Kingdom. It was thought to be the best and only reasonable option given the differences of opinions north and south.

And there, in a nutshell, is the reason for the ongoing and occasional violent uprisings in this country.

Northern Ireland was a majority Protestant country (around 65%) with, interestingly, a high percentage of evangelical Christians. The remaining 35%, Catholics and Nationalists, felt marginalised and isolated from their bigger southern counterpart.

However, believe me when I tell you that as a young man being raised in this tiny country with the short history on the edge of Europe, I have no recollection whatsoever of being taught or encouraged to 'hate' Catholics. On reflection back to those days, it's probable that more informed and intelligent political and social decisions by our so-called leaders would have avoided much, if not all, of what followed in the years to come.

The stories of your life, your experiences and your reaction to them, as I've already said, are always about perspective. Having a particular perspective doesn't render your viewpoint any less true or less correct than someone else's. It's just that your views are formed from a different position from that of the other person.

For me, my perspective was that I was just an ordinary young man living in a small country which I regarded as my own. My family had lived in this part of Ireland for over 300 years, as far as I could determine, and had every right to call it 'home'. Others who claimed a Republican heritage regarded me and every other Protestant living in Northern Ireland as their enemy and were doing everything within their power to destroy the country. They would kill innocent men, women and children without any remorse. They would destroy businesses and buildings to undermine and collapse the economy. If given half the chance, they would drive me and my family out of our homes and our city and our country. We were under attack and Irish Nationalist Terrorism was the evil aggressor.

Of course, other young men from the Catholic and Nationalist communities had similar perceptions, albeit diametrically opposite. They believed that they were being deliberately discriminated against, marginalised and oppressed by a foreign government that had neither the right nor the authority to govern them and who supported a corrupt and biased government in Northern Ireland to maintain the status quo. The agents of that oppression were these Ulster Scottish immigrants who didn't really belong to the country, no matter how long their generations had lived here.

The anger caused by this perceived injustice fuelled a desire for independence from Britain, the end to this contrived 'Northern Ireland' country, and the reunification of Ireland. In their view, the violence was perpetrated by the British state and needed an equally violent response. They were fighting for freedom from an oppressor and, whilst innocent people may be hurt or killed, it was entirely worth it to achieve the freedom that they desired.

Even as you read this you are liable to feel drawn to one or other of the above points of view. Your choice will be influenced by your own life, background and perspective. It's complicated, isn't it? By God's grace we have moved on from these intransigent and opposite positions, but the same story is being played out all over the world in Africa, the Middle East and Asia, and even closer to home in America and Europe.

Probably one of the hardest things for anyone to do is to see things from another's perspective. That's why we need the grace of the Holy Spirit to infuse our lives. If we can get God's righteous and just perspective and find His heart for situations and circumstances then we'll get closer to the Kingdom.

That's one of the challenges still facing us all in Ireland, to look back at events and circumstances and try to put ourselves in the position of the other point of view. If nothing else, it may assist our understanding, even if it doesn't excuse or fully explain.

So within the context of my perspective, several reactionary terrorist groups on the Protestant side of the fence were formed, essentially as a resistance to the threat of IRA violence. Rallies were held and recruitment drives organised to mobilise the Protestant population to action. Young men of all shapes and sizes would be recruited to fight in the ensuing struggle against the Irish Republican Army 'enemy'.

I remember leaving my house one summer's evening to walk a short distance to a sports club in a street about a quarter of a mile away. Somehow or other we'd learned that there was to be some sort of a display by one of these paramilitary groups in or around that spot. As I left I can distinctly remember my mother's words, "Don't go joining anything now, son."

"No, mum, I'm just going to have a look."

I remember those words clearly, and when I found myself a few minutes later watching a squad of around 40 or 50 masked men drilling in military fashion on the street outside the hall, they were still resonating in my mind.

Now it's possible that I would never have made any other decision in any case, or perhaps were it not for my mother's warning I might have made a monumentally wrong decision, but in any case, when the 'officer' marshalling and drilling the paramilitaries turned to me and said, "Do you want to join, son?" my reply was straightforward.

"No, I'm just watching."

I went home shortly afterwards.

Things got little better in the country in the months that followed and terrorist outrage heaped upon outrage. The siege mentality gripped us further and a new word became common in the streets where I lived – the vigilante.

In the midst of anarchy and trouble you can never be too sure how events and circumstances begin and are sustained. My recollection is that in streets and roads in Protestant areas of Belfast makeshift barriers were constructed and put in position across access roads into communities to keep the threat of the marauding IRA terrorist away from our homes and allow us to sleep safely in our beds. That's what I and my friends and family firmly believed.

Whatever the logic, I found myself standing behind one of those hastily constructed barricades with a wooden stick of some sort in one hand as a weapon and a scarf wrapped tightly around my face to disguise my identity. Perhaps I was ready to fight for my country; perhaps I was just along for the ride. Well, it was pretty exciting! There were a couple of dozen of us gathered there including a few of my close friends. We stood around in good humour, disorganised, ramshackle and almost playing at being our area's defenders. On recollection, I remember standing behind a structure made of bits of construction timber, hijacked cars and vans, rubbish bins and advertising hoardings erected about half a mile from where I lived and affording no protection whatsoever to my own particular house – but, hey, it was for the community!

The mood of the small crowd changed, however, when a British Army land rover approached the barricade. The problem was the street we had blocked was a reasonably major thorough-fare and couldn't be allowed to be closed off by a bunch of thugs!

A soldier got out and approached the barrier.

Now the thing is, the British soldier was our friend, of course. Having been sent here, initially, to watch over the Catholic population they soon found themselves victims of the advancing terrorism from part of that community and bearing the brunt of some appalling violence.

The loyalists, of which I was one, were supposed to support these guys.

The group fell silent.

"Sorry lads," said the squaddie, "but you're going to have to move this, so off you go and we'll clear it away."

A challenge! What would we do, stand and fight our case? Put up a defence and refuse to budge? Would we give up and leave? Well, a bit of both, actually. One by one the 'defenders' began to move away under the watchful eye of the army.

I was one of them. I remember taking off my mask, setting aside the large piece of wood which I had somehow decided was my weapon of choice should the IRA turn up, and walking back home.

A few did stay behind to make a stand against this perceived aggression and I later heard that things had degenerated into some violence. I also heard later that some of those who stayed had been recruited into one of the loyalist terrorist factions, in order to direct their ire at the appropriate enemy and not the soldiers, who never wanted to be in Belfast anyway. Some ended up in prison, some fell eventually into criminality and some, I suspect, were injured and killed in the remaining years of 'The Troubles'.

But, again, for whatever reason, I removed my scarf, set down the stick and walked home.

Now what's the point of these stories.

The point is that somewhere in everyone's walk of life, and in particular the future WARRIOR POETS, decisions are made, choices are selected and events occur that present some sort of fork in the road of our lives. We choose. Some of these are wise and good choices and result in good outcomes; some of these are awful choices and end up destroying people and lives. The point is that the most apparently insignificant and unrelated events go together with the big monumental ones to create the person you are.

But the counter point is this. Whatever decisions you made, whatever direction you chose, God is in the business of pursuing your heart in such a way that He can use us even after the most trying and troubled circumstances that could occur in our lives have happened. And use us to great effect. He can use a country like Northern Ireland and He can use an individual, no matter what their past or circumstances. If Cain had responded correctly, God would have used him in the most dynamic and exciting way.

All things can and will work together for good for those that love the Lord. Were you gifted when you were younger in an area that you've never developed? God knows and He can still use you. Have you no skills whatsoever but it appears that He is opening a door for you that is almost bizarrely opposite to your natural inclinations? He knows what He is doing.

The man that I am now and the impact, great or small, that I have, through God, managed to achieve, is all tied up with the places I have been, the experiences of my life and the choices that were made. He was at my shoulder when I stood as a foolish youth behind the barricade. He was whispering sense in my ear when I watched the paramilitary marching drills. All the changes in the growth of our church in Belfast have been episodes in which He is continually at work. He is building His worldwide Church, and the gates of hell will not prevail against it. His ways are higher than ours. He is in the business of taking lives that are ordinary, and turning them into lives that are extraordinary. He is seeking worshippers. He is seeking poets. He is seeking warriors. He was always in pursuit. He has a purpose for me and He has a purpose for you.

CHAPTER 10

Step Forward Warrior Poets

Although the phrase WARRIOR POETS has, I am told, been used fairly commonly in descriptions of the old Celtic legends and myths, I first came across it in the foreword to one of Erwin McManus' famously inspiring books. It was a dedication to his son and the simple phrase resonated with me at the time as he used it to describe the character of both himself and his boy, 'fellow WARRIOR POETS'.

There's something of an oxymoron about the phrase. Most of us would understand the nature and character of the 'warrior' as aggressive, bold, heroic and brave. At the same time, the few poets that we may know or have heard of often come across as slightly prim, mild-mannered and effete.

We wouldn't necessarily consider the two, the warrior and the poet, as having much in common.

Yet the poetic character of warriors is not that uncommon and has most recently been portrayed in film by soft-spoken, articulate, wild men like William Wallace, Rob Roy, Gandalf and others.

In real life, men like Tim Collins, a military man from Northern Ireland, whose famous 'call to battle' before the second Gulf War has apparently made it to the wall of the Oval Office in the White House are regarded with some considerable respect.

Some theologians have described David as a WARRIOR POET and, indeed, it was this biblical hero that Erwin had in mind, (he told me), when he used the phrase.

But, in this chapter, I'd like to draw you to a couple of other warriors. In particular, one named Barak and his 'queen' Deborah (she was actually one of the judges of Israel).

The story is found in Judges 4-5 and there are some striking lessons about worship and warfare, which are worth noting from this passage. These lessons, for me, bear heavily towards what it means to be a worshipper and a leader, and, perhaps serve as a base for the worship leaders ministry.

Many of you reading this book will have a desire to combine the natural gift that you may have in areas of the creative arts with a desire to present an acceptable offering of worship to God. As far as I can see, you, under God's grace, are the WARRIOR POETS of the 21st Century.

You will have no doubt heard that we are in the midst of what is called a postmodern society. As far as I understand it, one of the resultant core changes in a postmodern society is reckoned to be a turning away from the logical, scientific and industrial mindset and a move towards spirituality, community and relationships. This is mirrored in society, apparently, by a disaffection with the perception that the most valuable and usable asset that you might have is information, knowledge and learning and the ability to transmit that to others. (Hence the rapid rise of information technology and the multi-million dollar businesses built around it.)

But consider this – information is now old news. IT and its multi-faceted world of communication and transfer of information is getting old. Your granny is now on the web and she knows how to use it! Maybe in this apparently postmodern society something else is beginning to re-emerge and have a greater impact on our society.

Creativity

Perhaps the next big boom is creativity. Erwin certainly thinks so. Perhaps those that find the apparently hidden gem of real and exciting creativity in their expression and output will take the world by storm. Let's consider this, at least. Our God is a Creator God, and He made us in His image. Therefore, one of our highest and most productive skills must be to create – to do new things, to make new music, to furnish new ideas and concepts, to take formless materials and make some aesthetically pleasing or useful product. To be creative.

Let's look at Judges 4:1-8, and the story of Barak and Deborah:

After Ehud died, the Israelites once again did evil in the eyes of the LORD. So the LORD sold them into the hands of Jabin, a king of Canaan, who reigned in Hazor. The commander of his army was Sisera, who lived in Harosheth Haggoyim. Because he had nine hundred iron chariots and had cruelly oppressed the Israelites for twenty years, they cried to the LORD for help. Deborah, a prophetess, the wife of Lappidoth, was leading Israel at that time. She held court under the Palm of Deborah between Ramah and Bethel in the hill country of Ephraim, and the Israelites came to her to have their disputes decided. She sent for Barak son of Abinoam from Kedesh in Naphtali and said to him, 'The LORD, the God of Israel, commands you: "Go, take with you ten thousand men of Naphtali and Zebulun and lead the way to Mount Tabor. I will lure Sisera, the commander of Jabin's army, with his chariots and his troops to the Kishon River and give him into your hands. . . . Barak said to her, 'If you go with me, I will go; but if you don't go with me, I won't go.'

At first glance, this is the start of a simple historical story of a long gone battle, millennia past and lost in terms of its impact on us. But here's the thing about the Bible. I continue to find that the depth and layers behind the contents of this wonderful Book are absolutely endless. There is truth upon truth and wisdom upon wisdom in every chapter and page. There is nothing accidental or irrelevant in it. As Bishop Graham Cray said, the Bible exhibits 'astonishing consistency' in its narrative. [2]

We want to concentrate on the character and actions of the WARRIOR POET, Barak alongside his WARRIOR POET 'queen', Deborah. So, what can we draw from this first part of the passage?

Firstly, how do we know that Barak was a warrior?

Well, the name Barak means 'Thunderbolt'. Now, correct me if I'm wrong, but you don't go wandering around ancient tribal civilisations with a name like Thunderbolt and be a bit of a wimp. If I ever decide to become a superhero, I shall call myself Thunderbolt.

Someone with the name Thunderbolt is strong, fast, shocking, powerful and frightening. Thunderbolt is the name of a warrior (or, a superhero, perhaps).

Secondly, as we will eventually discover as the chapter unfolds, he ultimately did win the battle that he was called to. The fact is he won an amazing victory, on foot, against an army of stronger well-equipped oppressors who happened to have 900 iron chariots in their ranks. Some historians would suggest that the Israelites were not particularly great horsemen and generally fought as infantry or foot soldiers. Assuming that to be true, for the moment, (though it doesn't quite add up in other biblical stories), Barak won a quite incredible victory against a significantly more mobile and armed oppressor, and, such was the victory that he won, he is listed among the 'heroes of the faith' in the book of Hebrews. So we have established him as a warrior of some reputation.

Then, how do we know he was a poet or why should we consider him as such?

Well, firstly, he wrote a song with Deborah. It's there in Judges 5. I know the pages of our Bible label it as the *Song of Deborah* but for sure there was collaboration between Deborah and Barak, probably most clearly expressed in verse 12, but also supported by the first verse of that same chapter when it announces that Deborah and Barak sang the song together.

What a sight that must have been. The Israeli army returning to camp having won a decisive and all-consuming victory over their oppressor of 20 years, God's handiwork obvious in the experience. Perhaps a few battle scars and wounds to brag about on the return. The air palpable with the sense of victory, camp fires burning and casting a glow upon the tents of the encampment, wine flowing, food aplenty and riches and booty taken from the enemy.

Think of the most dramatic post-battle scene from *The Lord of the Rings* or *Braveheart*, or some other movie you may have seen and you can get something of a feel for what must have been taking place.

Israel, long oppressed and poverty stricken, now free and wealthy. Music, shouting, cheering, noise and clamour.

Then a cry goes up, "Come and sing to us, Barak and Deborah, of this great victory."

And so, standing to their feet with the acclamation of thousands of bruised, bloodied but victorious tribal warriors, they sing a song of victory, and praise and celebration.

Bet you wish you had been there.

There is a further reason why we can assume that this warrior, Barak, had something of the poet within his blood. It's in his heritage.

To understand a little of this we need to go back to Genesis 49 where we read how the old patriarch, Jacob, is 'naming' his sons. It was a ceremony where he was speaking over each son, identifying their strengths and also outlining their future. With each son, Jacob speaks a prophetic word relevant to the calling on their lives. These prophetic words are not just explanations of the names that each son was given at birth. In fact, the words differ dramatically from the translation and meaning of their names. The whole chapter presents the details of this re-naming process and the words spoken over them.

There are some great words spoken by the elderly patriarch, "Judah, you will defeat your enemies; Reuben, you are first in the list of rank and honour; Benjamin is a wolf that prowls." Stirring stuff!

What about Naphtali, Barak's tribe? What was to be their given character?

"Naphtali is a deer set free, that bears beautiful fawns" (Genesis 49:21).

Oops.

Hardly the stuff of warriors or poets, don't you think. I don't know what a deer set free conjures up in your mind but, to me, it paints a picture of prancing and dancing and gambolling around in not a particularly macho way!

The New International Version of the Bible offers an alternative translation of the second

part of the verse and suggests we could read it as, "Naphtali is a deer set free, he utters beautiful words."

Now that is more interesting, "he utters beautiful words." Is this a picture that suggests that the Naphtalites would be known for their beautiful words, for their expression, maybe even (because of the 'deer' thing) for their dancing? Barak's heritage was in a tribe who did not have the characteristics of a warrior, but the characteristics of a poet.

So here we have this unusual, but not uncommon mix, the WARRIOR POET.

What can we learn from this WARRIOR POET that can teach us something about worship?

Probably one of the most intriguing verses in the passage is verse 8. Barak is asked by God, through Deborah, to go and fight the battle and in his reply to this request he says: "If you go with me I will go, but if you don't go with me, I won't go."

What state of mind was Barak in when he said this? Remember that culturally the role of women in the society that Barak and Deborah were a part of was not normally in a place of leadership or authority, but rather in a servant role, deferring to the male. Yet here is Barak, asking for the company of Deborah, before he would go to the battle.

His warrior status is undoubted, perhaps it was living with the expectation of a name like Thunderbolt under the cosh of a malevolent dictator like Sisera, that had broken his confidence.

Whatever it was, Barak was desperately honest in this request. And here is our first lesson.

People, we need to be honest in all we do. We need to act with integrity and be true to the gifts that God has given us and the experience of our lives. Writers, we need to write songs that are not derivative, or mimic styles and forms of the latest musical expression in the secular field. We need to be at the forefront of creativity in this world.

If there's one thing that the world can see through and has little time for, it's falsehood and duplication. Our worship needs the power and dynamism of truth. Jesus said we must worship in spirit and truth, and this is our call. Let's not be afraid to be true. True to our God and true to ourselves.

I understand that the bookshelves of our stores, including Christian Bookstores, are filled with a plethora of self-help materials designed to help us get over some recent or distant traumatic circumstance. Books designed to help and improve our self-image, forget our past, and move swiftly towards some more exciting and dynamic future. These are all good things; indeed, I have read and benefited from a number of these writings myself.

But, sometimes I wonder if there may be some other, possibly greater, benefit in a holy acceptance of who we are, of what has happened to us, of the circumstances that have made us the person we are now and to embrace what has happened. I suspect that not everyone can do that, or would even be expected to. Some of the hurt and abuses in our past are necessary areas for the healing of God's Holy Spirit. Perhaps there are some who can and should embrace their past. Some who can acknowledge that all things do work together for good. Some who can echo the words of Graham Kendrick's song, Lord You've been good to me, all my life. Your loving kindness never fails, and with rejoicing, go forward.

Perhaps these are the WARRIOR POETS.

Have you ever heard of dog and cat theology? I can't lay claim to this thought process, someone passed it on to me during a conversation some months back, but it's worth repeating.

A dog sees its master return at the end of the working day.

And the dog thinks, "This guy looks after me, he plays with me, he feeds me, he gives me somewhere to sleep, he's always there for me and he cares for me. He keeps me safe and I want for nothing.

He must be God!"

A cat, however, sees its master return at the end of the working day. And the cat thinks, "This guy looks after me, he plays with me, he feeds me, he gives me somewhere to sleep, he's always there for me and he cares for me. He keeps me safe and I want for nothing. I must be God!"

This world doesn't need any more cat theology in our songs and lifestyles and ambitions. Rather, it needs the expression of worship from thankful hearts that are honest and true to the people we are and the calling on our lives. How much do you think King David's experiences came through in the Psalms he wrote?

The Lord is my Shepherd; O Lord, the king rejoices in Your strength; Have mercy upon me, O God, according to your loving kindness. These three and dozens of other songs that he wrote were reflections of both spiritual truth and personal truth.

So Barak is a desperately honest man.

Secondly, Barak at this time was a fragile man.

Anyone involved in the creative process will always open themselves up to criticism. It goes with the territory. Everyone has an opinion, and everyone is entitled to that opinion. But, I imagine we'll all agree, criticism is hard to take sometimes and so we react badly, or get defensive. We feel fragile.

Well, here's the thing. It's good to be fragile, particularly in the area of worship and creativity. Sometimes God will call you to be broken and fragile, for the sake of a broken world. Sometimes you cannot be used by God, unless you are right at the end of what you think are your own abilities and need to rely totally on Him.

Honesty and Fragility

In the last chapter I gave some small insights into a few occasions in my life's journey, both on a personal level and in the context of my country, that probably shaped the person that I now am. Most of the songs that I have written which have made any impact in our church or beyond were ones which came out of those and other similar experiences and occasions. Incidents in our land, in our church, and in my life have, on reflection, formed the core of worship songs which God has seen fit to use the most.

In other words, the honest songs, often not as finely crafted or grammatically sound as some others I have composed, were those that resonated with God's worshippers. In fact, the other songs, and there are many, which I have composed to fill a gap, or for a special occasion or as a simple muse, have generally disappeared without trace, like Cain's unacceptable offering. Writers who I have spent some time with like Matt Redman, Paul Baloche, and others would share very similar thoughts.

The third thing verse 8 tells us is that Barak was in a relationship that he honoured.

Remember, as we have said, the status of women at this time in history should have been the entire opposite of what was happening here. Here we have the warrior, broken and bruised, seeking the comfort, solace and companionship of his queen, Deborah.

In verse 9, after Barak asks her to go with him, Deborah agrees, but speaks prophetically into the situation by telling Barak that he would receive no honour as a result of the battle, for the Lord's victory would be at the hands of a woman.

Some commentators regard this verse as evidence of Deborah scolding Barak or chiding him for his state of mind and the comment he made. But, I really don't think so. Remember what I said before, if the Bible doesn't say it, it isn't there. There is no record of Barak responding to these words. It seems that he accepted what was said and moved on.

Barak was delivered a statement of fact by Deborah. He wasn't judged or punished. All that happened was that his glory went to another. Barak was not afraid to let his glory go to another.

Don't be afraid to let your glory go to another. In fact, prefer one another in Jesus' name. The recipient of the glory for whatever actions you're called by God to perform, is of no consequence to you.

I have a very good friend called Arlen Salte who runs a worship event called Breakforth in Edmonton, Canada, in the depths of winter. Against all the odds, the conference is a major success. As many as 10,000 people turn up for what has become the largest worship conference in North America. Ten years ago he began with around 200 people and now thousands of folks make there way to the event each year.

Few people have ever heard of Arlen. He is not one of the 'big names' in worship music or creative arts. He quietly goes about his business, often invisible, but at most giving the announcements during the meetings and honouring those who visit and volunteer to help the event run smoothly. I rarely hear anyone honour him.

He is a WARRIOR POET and he is happy to let his glory go to another.

Ultimately, the glory always goes to Christ.

By the way, perhaps you are a Deborah in the life of some Barak somewhere. You are close to one of these struggling creative types who are wracked with insecurities and uncertainties about their abilities and calling, and they choose to offload the doubts, fears and problems that they encounter in their walk on you. If that's the case, please be a Deborah. Be prepared to listen, to encourage, to support, and to go with them into the battle. Always be ready to remind them that whatever they do, they do it all for the glory of the One who sent them.

Barak was an honest, fragile man in relationship, and this relationship was crucial to his success. He took up the challenge, went with his queen to the battlefield, rallied his troops, fought the battle and won.

There are some more lessons to learn in this latter part of the passage from verses 10-16. These are lessons about the battle we, as WARRIOR POETS, are called to fight.

Barak summoned the tribes of Zebulun and Naphtali. Ten thousand men followed him, and Deborah also went with him. Now Heber the Kenite had left the other Kenites, the descendants of Hobab, Moses' brother-in-law, and pitched his tent by the great tree in Zaanannim near Kedesh. When they told Sisera that Barak son of Abinoam had gone up to Mount Tabor, Sisera gathered together his nine hundred iron chariots and all the men with him, from Harosheth Haggoyim to the Kishon River. Then Deborah said to Barak, 'Go! This is the day the LORD has given Sisera into your hands. Has not the LORD gone ahead of you?' So Barak went down Mount Tabor, followed by ten thousand men. At Barak's advance, the LORD routed Sisera and all his chariots and army by the sword, and Sisera abandoned his chariot and fled on foot. But Barak pursued the chariots and army as far as Harosheth Haggoyim. All the troops of Sisera fell by the sword; not a man was left.

Following God's instructions, spoken to him by Deborah, Barak had called together his fellow dancing deer of Naphtali and another tribe called Zebulun.

The thing about a battle, particularly against an enemy as powerful and ruthless as Sisera, is that you definitely want to take your best fighters and most skilful combatants into the battlefield. Given the Naphtalites are known for their prancing around like deer set free, and their inordinate ability with beautiful words, you might think that it would be a good idea to have a few of those warrior tribes like Judah and Reuben and Benjamin to take with you into the battle.

But, for some reason, God decides that Barak should take the tribe of Zebulun with him.

Back in Genesis 49 again, how does Jacob describe this particular tribe and their natural skills and inclinations? What characteristic will they have that will make them most suited for the task ahead? The answer is found in verse 13, "Zebulun will live by the seashore."

Great! The other tribe called by God to fight the land battle were a bunch of sailors, harbour masters, and beach bums!

The truth is, in the eyes of the world and probably in the eyes of experts in land battle strategy, these were the wrong people with whom to go into battle! Sailors, dancers and poets. I can just imagine, prior to the battle, the interviewer from the local TV station in Israel speaking to the head of strategic military studies from the University of Judea.

"Professor Ichabod, Sir, what's your opinion on the strategy employed by Queen Deborah and Barak for this very strategic and long-awaited battle?"

"Well, in short, Bob, it's the most ridiculous thing I have ever heard. There are hundreds of thousands of fighting men in Israel with a great tradition of battle skills just waiting to take up arms against the oppressor. They are ready, willing and able. These guys are going in with a bunch of dancers and the merchant navy. It is doomed to failure."

(He might even have said something like, "What can you expect from a woman," but we'd best not go there.)

Do you believe that God has a sense of humour? In verse 14, the Bible describes how the men are positioned on the slopes of Mount Tabor before the battle commences. We can guess that the band of brothers assembled were not really relishing the fight that would soon come. But they were ready to go.

Have you ever started running down a hill and found that once you started you couldn't stop? Have you ever felt the abject fear of your legs powering along at two or three times faster than they were ever designed to travel as you gain speed? Can you imagine the motley collection of Naphtalite artists and Zebulunite boatmen standing on the slopes, not particularly well armed given they were oppressed for 20 years and wondering how on earth they were going to do this, charging at incredible speed down the slopes of Mount Tabor probably screaming their heads off?

These were, in the eyes of all sensible observers, the wrong people for the job. But not in God's eyes. He uses the foolish of this world to confound the wise.

They were running so fast, they caught up and passed the chariots of Sisera. They annihilated the oppressor. In the end, they won a total and complete victory.

Don't ever make the mistake of assuming that because all your skills don't seem to fit the sensible and logical gifting required for a task, that God cannot use you, particularly in the area of worship.

We were all made to worship, we are all used by God in worship.

One further part of the passage could almost be missed. Yet it has one of the most significant messages for the WARRIOR POETS of this generation in the few words that it uses.

It's in verse 15 and the phrase is, "When Barak advanced."

You see, up until this point Barak had received the call of God, followed by the promise of God for victory, supported by his helpmate for the venture, Deborah. His 10,000 unlikely heroes were in place, they were on the mount that God had called them to, they were ready.

But until Barak placed one foot in front of the other and advanced, nothing was ever going to happen. Until he moved, God was not going to move.

What will God do with you, if you take that step?

For Barak, everything was in place, but he needed to make the first move.

For the call of God on your life, everything is in place. God knows the purposes that He has for you. You are surrounded by all the right people. They might look all wrong! They might seem entirely inappropriate, but God has brought you to this mountain and He's waiting for you to advance.

He knows where you've come from and He knows your history. Who could imagine what God can do with you? You are one of those whom Jesus has pursued and captured with His love. He has restored the worshipping relationship again that was previously lost.

Whatever step you take in your call, He will always move. Barak saw and rejoiced in the results, even though the honour did not go to him. You may, in turn, not receive any honour either, like Barak. You may not even see what God will do, but no matter, what you can be sure of is that He will move.

Many years ago I was asked to lead worship at a men's conference in Belfast, which in a short while became the largest annual gathering of Christian men in the United Kingdom. In the early days we faced this issue of styles and types of songs head-on, as the men who would come were drawn from every denomination of the body of Christ.

For the sake of worship, I tried to combine and blend as many new songs and old songs and hymns and choruses over the day to satisfy all attendees. My main concern was that we would worship together and that the choice of music would not be a hindrance but a help. At the end of the event I have to admit that I fully expected a few negative reactions from some of those who gathered, and as I stood on the platform when the meeting ended, I awaited the response.

I saw him, firstly, out of the corner of my eye, purposefully approaching the stage. He was dressed in a denim jacket and jeans and had what we called a 'skinhead' haircut back then. Only the toughest of the tough could sport a skinhead cut. He looked unhappy as he made his way up the stairs at the side of the stage area and onto the platform, making a beeline for yours truly.

I actually stood sideways as he came close. (I read that in a book somewhere about protecting yourself.) I thought he was going to hit me. He was a tough, hard looking character. We stood face to face (ish!). He spoke.

"Did you write, *Not by Might?*"

(Gulp) "Yes."

"Could I just say ..." he paused here for a moment, and glanced down. "Could I just say that my wife died about a year ago and I have been so depressed that I have thought many times about committing suicide and ending it all. But that song and your music has saved my life."

I was speechless. I felt like a jerk.

His eyes filled up momentarily with tears, and being the hard guy that he was, without another word he turned and walked quickly off the stage. I stood dumbfounded. It was not what I had expected at all.

Never ever underestimate what God can do with a heart given over to worship and serve Him. Never ever be afraid to let Him have all the glory and honour and for you to take nothing. God can save lives through what you might do.

I know practically every worship leader, writer, artist, actor, dancer, painter will have similar stories to tell and mine is no different from many. So don't think anything of me in its telling. Just decide now that when God says, "advance", you will take that step for Him.

Finally, a last word of encouragement for all you WARRIOR POETS out there who have made it this far.

And, I suppose another indication of the depths of the wisdom of this Book that we call the Bible, the Holy Word of God.

Do you know what the tribal area called Naphtali eventually became? If you have a map or two at the back of your Bible you can have a look. If you sneak a peek at Isaiah 9, you can also get a clue.

Naphtali became Galilee.

And although Jesus' tribe was Judah, one of the warrior tribes, He was also known as the Man of Galilee. He was a Man of integrity and honesty who spoke the truth unfailingly and unswervingly, true to His character and His calling.

He was a fragile Man, despised, rejected and prone to tears for lost souls and lost friends.

He was a Man who spoke beautiful words. Words that calmed the storm, raised the dead, banished demons, calmed the multitudes, made children laugh, spoke away sin, encouraged the downhearted. A Man who spoke the greatest words of love and life ever heard or recorded.

A Man who valued His friends. A Man who laid down His life for His friends.

A Man whose desire and purpose was not for His own honour, but that all the glory would go to His Father in heaven. A Man who set out to restore that relationship between a Father and His children. A Man who told the errant thief at the cross that He would be bringing him back to Paradise.

A Man who fought a battle. A battle against the very wrath of hell itself. One whose beatings and wounds rendered Him unrecognisable to His friends and was so disfiguringly abused that people had to turn their face away.

But One who won the greatest of victories, even over death itself, and opened the gates to Paradise and communion with His Father.

Is Jesus our WARRIOR POET? Is the Lord Jesus our great WARRIOR POET?

I believe so.

Will you take up the challenge and call of the WARRIOR POET?

Listen, who is going to reach this lost world?

In the UK, a so-called Christian nation, less than 7% of the population claim to be active Christians. In France and other European countries the percentage is as low as 1%. Great Britain has the highest divorce rate in Europe. An area close to where I live has the highest percentage of single parent families in Europe. In 1991 in England there were 12 million prescriptions issued for anti-depressants. In 2001 it was 24 million. One child dies from AIDS in Africa every 3 seconds. In the world today 1 billion people earn less than $1 per day in slave-like jobs. Around three thousand people per day still die of starvation in this world of surplus. Women and children are oppressed and abused by religious and political structures through the developed and developing world.

This world needs salvation as it has never needed it before.

Who's going to lift up the name of Jesus Christ in worship and present Him to this world again? Who is going to reach the nations with the saving grace of Christ?

Perhaps, it's you, broken, dispirited and feeling unfit for the task.

Perhaps, it's you, WARRIOR POET of the 21st Century.

[2] Quoted from a presentation to UK worship writers in November 2003

CHAPTER 11
The Days of Elijah Story:
Part 1 - Can Creativity Really Have an Impact?

Whenever I pick up a book by any writer, one of the things that really turns me off is if they use the body of their text to present some sort of creative utterance of their own, (or some close friend or relative)! Yes, I realise it's weird, but finding a poem stuck in the middle of the text which was penned by their great uncle Dilbert, or whatever, just doesn't do it for me.

So here I am, writing a chapter where the core of the entire passage is my own song.

I am really sorry! All I can say is, forgive me! And please bear with me. I think and hope it might be worth it. I want to try and share something of what God can do with your particular creative gift and background in advancing His kingdom. I want to under-score the role of the WARRIOR POET.

The song is *Days of Elijah*.

If you haven't heard of it, it's written out in full at the end of the next chapter. Skip over to the words if you need to. And if you want to hear the best recorded version, grab either the Brooklyn Tabernacle Choir's version or that by Judi Jacobs.

Of all the songs I have ever penned, this is the one that draws the greatest reaction from both within and outside the Church. My wife, Jacqueline, calls it my 'one hit wonder'. As I said before, people write additional verses for it and send them to me. I get letters and emails asking everything from what it basically is all about to whether I am a pre- or post-millennialist. A number of books have gone to print with less than complimentary comments about it. Apparently some feel it has too much imagery, too many references to the Bible, (I couldn't figure that either), is inappropriate for worship and impossible for 'ordinary' people to understand.

One commentator inferred that I had just grabbed some names from the Scriptures and stuck them in randomly. He even went as far as to add a few bizarre and obscure references himself. Ah, the slings and arrows!

The thing is, and this is the point I want to get across in this section, I freely admit that the song is unusual and different and that it probably falls outside of the worship genre for a lot of people – if such a thing exists. And, despite being 'Mr Sensitive' and feeling occasionally aggrieved at the more unpleasant comments, I'm pretty much OK with it all.

It has become the most loved and most sung of all my writings. The letters and emails from people describing how it changed their personal and corporate worship perspective, and, interestingly, how they didn't find it that difficult to figure out, far outweigh the negatives. Actually, the ordinary people find it perfectly OK. It's the smart guys that seem to have a problem. I have been told of non-Christians coming to faith directly and indirectly through the song. I had one very nice lady tell me that it had made her start to actually pay attention to what she sang. (If that can be repeated throughout the worldwide Church we will definitely have gotten somewhere.) It has been translated into over 40 languages, including Indonesian, Cantonese, Nepalese, Inuit and Japanese. It is cross-cultural, cross-generational and international.

And yet, if you asked me to sit down and write another song in a similar form, or even add an extra verse or two myself, I very much doubt that I could do so.

This is where all the 'how-to's' and 'do's and don'ts' that we resort to in our songwriting fall apart. We're encouraged to write poetically, but not too poetically; make sure our doctrine is correct, but try to avoid any contentious theological pitfalls; make happy-clappy rhythms match upbeat songs and melodic ballads express contemplative worship; use 'now' language but don't dumb down too much, and so on and so forth.

I reckon that by the time we get to the totally politically correct, non-mysterious, happening, relevant, complex but not too complex words and tune, we've probably forgotten what we were writing for in the first place!

So, here is, perhaps, another take on it all.

Firstly, I have come to understand that there are two types

of worship song writer. Both types are 'gifted' in the sense that, (although practically everyone can write a song or a poem if pushed), they both have natural God-given ability to find melody and lyrical poetry. They can both put together words and tunes in such a way as to make it possible for others to engage in communal singing and, hopefully, sung worship.

But there's a difference between the two types.

One is driven by the pursuit of song writing and music as a career or specific calling. Their heart's desire is solely to be a writer of music, poetry and song. Any other career or job is merely a means to support this primary purpose and perhaps provide an income while they fulfil this higher calling. Sometimes they might even deny themselves their basic needs and, to others, appear totally reckless in their attitude and lifestyle, just for the sake of their art. They are the traditional 'starving artist', if you like.

The other is a responder to stimulation.

Circumstances, situations and experiences that happen around them inspire their creative juices and they only write when they feel the need. Someone might, for example, pen a secret poem to express their thoughts to a loved one in the throes of romantic entanglement, but never write anything else again. They don't see themselves as writers by profession, but are pleased to allow their creativity to burst forth when inspiration comes.

To put a biblical handle on it, the first is rather like an Asaph.

1 Chronicles 15:17 is one of the first mentions of Asaph who is chosen and appointed by the Levites, at David's instruction, as a musical director. His initial role seems to have been to sound the cymbals, which might not appear to be a particularly auspicious first step, but by chapter 16:5, he is described as the leader of the worship group at the Ark of the Covenant.

We find him again as the author of several of the Psalms, including the majestic Psalm 73.

Probably the greatest accolade that he is afforded in the Scriptures is the simple but profound phrase in Nehemiah 12:46.

Nehemiah has rebuilt the walls of the city of Jerusalem and assists in restoring worship in the temple with the Israelites who have managed to return to their homeland from captivity. Leaders of music, priests and worshippers were once again directed to perform the functions appropriate to making a worship offering to the Lord. To clarify his understanding of the reasons for the ceremony taking place, Nehemiah says this:

"For long ago, in the days of David and Asaph, there had been directors for the singers and for the songs of praise and thanksgiving to God." (Nehemiah 12:46)

The people of Israel had spent 70 years in captivity and perhaps two generations had never had the opportunity to worship their God at the most holy site of the temple in Jerusalem. This was a monumental occasion for the remnant that had returned to the city. Nehemiah indicates how distant the memory is by the plaintive, almost story-like, phrase "long ago". You can almost imagine the tale being told to Israelite children beginning with the phrase, "Once upon a time, long, long ago, there were Worship Leaders in Jerusalem!" But Nehemiah's fleeting memory notes two names associated with the glory days of continuous worship in the temple, David and Asaph.

The shepherd king and Psalmist of Israel, side by side with the cymbal crasher! There is much that can be drawn from the story of Asaph, and we will look at this in another chapter, but it's safe to say that his calling was a career ministry as a Musician/ Writer and that, from small beginnings, he became recognised as a gifted Psalmist, even worthy of association with the king.

But there are also plenty of examples of the second responder type of writer in the Scriptures. The responder is a little like a Hannah, our friend Deborah or a Moses. Skilled for sure, but brought to the place of expressing God's worship because of an event or circumstance, and not really renowned for their creative abilities elsewhere.

The story of Hannah is right at the beginning of 1 Samuel. To paraphrase the text, Hannah really wants a child, but is unable to conceive. She loves her husband dearly but the intensity of the desire for a baby is overwhelming and all-consuming. Year after year on her regular visits to the tabernacle in Shiloh to perform an act of worship, she seeks God's provision. Finally, in her desperation, she makes a promise to God to dedicate the child to Him, if He will only grant her request.

Not long after this particular act of worship, (which is really what her promise to God is), she conceives and, in the fulness of time, gives birth to a baby boy whom she names Samuel, meaning heard by, or asked of God. In her unrestrained joy she writes and sings a staggering song of worship, written down for us in 1 Samuel 2. It has come to be known as 'Hannah's Song'.

Again, much could be said of the impact in the future of this entire act of worship. Samuel was instrumental, under God's guidance, in choosing David as the king and the lineage that David continued eventually gave way to the birth of Jesus. But I want us to note that there is no record of Hannah's other writings, nor of her becoming a recognised psalmist in the community. She wrote out of the fulness of her, truly gifted heart in response to her circumstances and experience. Millions have shared and sung of her experience over the many centuries between her time on earth and ours.

Why would this be important?

As best as I can say it, it's OK to be a working songwriter. In fact, it's more than OK, it's a very fine calling and one which has been demonstrated time after time by men and women like Isaac Watts, Charles Wesley, Fanny Crosby and many others.

The Church has been blessed for millennia by writers and composers ranging from the earthy, gracious passion of John Newton to the classical excellence of Handel. Men and women whose lives were given to their art and of whom we could say,

"Long ago there were hymn writers in the church, like Wesley and Crosby." If that's your call, then pursue it as you feel led.

However, for me, the excellent structure and pattern of the well-crafted song, the fine choice of phrasing and melody designed and selected to ensure that the song rises to crescendo at just the right time, the poetic perfection of the written word, whilst these are important, they are no better or superior to the explosive cry of the repentant, awe-inspired heart, expressing in the only words it knows the joy and glory of an encounter with the risen Christ. You write a worship song as an act of worship, and an act of worship is an offering to the revealed person of God.

No matter how skilled, how excellent, how all-encompassing, how relevant, how grammatical or how pleasing to the intellect of the critic a piece of writing may be, it is surely empty of merit if it hasn't been forged in the furnace of the hearts exposure to the glory and reality of the King of kings and Lord of lords.

I would gladly forfeit poetic excellence, appropriate structure, and dignified relevant cadence and content to feel my heart dragged by the passion of the songwriter into the presence of the Holy One of Israel.

While I am ranting on, let me say this.

Please, please, if I have to read one more pseudo-critic berate Matt Redman's glorious song *Undignified* with possibly well-intentioned but deeply depressing criticism just because it includes the phrase, "Na, na, na, na, na, hey!", I think I might scream! A manly scream, of course.

How difficult can it be to understand that the same David who wrote the most beautiful introductory line to a song, ever, "The Lord is my Shepherd, I shall not want", was probably bounding and dancing like an idiot as he brought the Ark into Jerusalem. No doubt, the phrase in the Scriptures – "much shouting" (2 Samuel 6:15) – which describes his entrance would not necessarily refer to a pleasant recitation of one of his Psalms.

No, he was probably screaming his head off. He may even have been singing, "Na, na, na, na, na, na, hey!"

We are in danger of sterilising the very passion of worship in our pursuit of some irrelevant classification of quality when it comes to songwriting. In deference to A W Tozer who said it first, the Church is at its coldest, most lifeless place when we replace relationship with ritual.

So, what sort of a writer might you be? Remember the questions from chapter 7? Well, here they are again:

1. If the only person to hear my songs, to hear my sermons, to hear my talks, to see me dance, to look at my paintings, or whatever, if that only person was God, would that be sufficient? If no one else heard the songs that you write, would it be entirely sufficient that you were able to sing them to God?

2. Can God really open doors that no man can shut? (Well, of course, He can and He can also shut doors that no man can open. But do you accept this fact and can you live in the grace and goodness of it?) Do we all understand that what we give, we give to Him alone and what happens after that is nothing to do with us and all to do with Him?

3. Finally, have you ever said, "God has told me that my songs/ sermon/ writings/ artwork are very important and it is essential that I get maximum exposure because the Church really, really needs to see and hear my stuff?"

Remember, I said the proper answers were: Yes, Yes, No.

If you answered 'yes' to the third question, then you might regard yourself as a 'career' type songwriter. But, you really, really have to guard your heart.

Before anyone gets angry, let me say this. We're not just writing songs here. For sure, if you feel you are gifted as a writer, you write in order that others might read! You sing in order that someone might listen. That's fine, that's a career choice. That's OK. But what a worship songwriter is doing is, rather, expressing worship in the form of a written song.

There's a difference.

The worship song is the natural gifting that is used by the writer to express his love and adoration to God. The song's entire purpose, for me, must be to express our heart to our Father and the Son. If someone else sings it with you, that's a bonus. If you're fortunate to have some people in a small group setting who will sing your songs in worship, that's a blessing bonus! If your church owns it and sings it, that's a double blessing bonus. But if the only one that sings it is you, in the solitude of your room, to the audience of One, that's enough. That's more than enough.

As far as I can ascertain from the great writers through the ages, their primary purpose was to express something of their thankfulness to God. Sometimes they felt the need to write in forms and styles that the ordinary people could sing, like the Wesley's and John Newton. Sometimes they pursued greater poetic quality, like Isaac Watts. Sometimes they wrote with an additional purpose of reaching men and women for God, like William Booth.

But I am entirely convinced that they cared little whether their songs were sung anywhere else, or achieved any recognition above the act of sacrificial worship that happened as they were written.

Here's a test, a test that happened naturally for me.

Let someone else promote and advance your songwriting. (By that I don't mean go and ask someone to do it!) If what you write is to have an impact way beyond your current frame of reference, why not let the Lord inspire someone who knows you to promote that on your behalf.

It might not happen. But if God has purpose for your creativity, then it will happen.

In the early days of my worship leading in Christian Fellowship Church, Belfast, around 1989/90, I had written some songs and we as a congregation were singing them. Because we were a relatively new and, by that time, small to mid-sized church, people felt free to let me know what they thought were good, and not so good, songs of worship. There was good relational input, and plenty of 'tough love'.

Paul Reid, my pastor, vetoed and considered every new submission and, despite his protestations to the contrary now, was never shy in suggesting when a new song should be laid aside. He usually made his feelings known halfway through the song by stroking his outstretched index finger across his throat in that well-known slicing motion. "Cut!" (By the way, just a note for some of you aspiring worship leaders, whenever he did so, as far as I was concerned the song was finished. He was and still is the Senior Pastor and God has set him in that role and responsibility for a good purpose. So always do, under God, what your Pastor tells you – submit to one another in love!)

One weekend a worship conference was organised in the city by another fellowship who, for convenience and size, used our facility. The visiting worship leader was a hero of mine called Dave Fellingham. In my opinion, one of the men used by God in the early renewal days to restore the heart of worship in Europe and a wonderful mentor to an emerging generation of songwriters, (including his own children).

Two very good friends, Stephen Doherty and John Willis, found out what hotel he was staying in and did two things. Firstly, they supplied him with a tape of my songs and then arranged that we would meet over lunch on one of the days around the conference. I had no input at all, I was not even aware of their actions. They felt that I had something graced within me and it needed to be shared.

In a way, it was pretty mean! Dave had to listen to the songs out of sheer politeness, really, as when I would be dragged in to meet him by my supporters, he would have to be able to say something!

When the day came I was jostled over to the hotel to meet him. I was embarrassed and felt a little stupid. I did not want to be there. This man was my hero, for goodness sake, let me worship from afar, brothers. My eager compatriots were highly charged and completely compelling. Dave had just finished a pretty gruelling weekend of speaking and seminars and was probably tired, wanting to get home, and spiritually spent. I was the last person on earth he wanted to see, I reckon.

We all, as is often the case, partook of lunch with some polite conversation and chit-chat. Time was moving on and around about coffee time, (which for us is normally the last part of a meal), my friends could hold it in no longer.

"Well, Dave, what did you think of his songs...?"

Ground, swallow me up.

A very tired but gracious David Fellingham said the following:

Robin, the songs are fine, they're OK. But one day you will write a song that will change everything. It will change your life, change other's lives and change the Church. But you haven't written it yet.

Well. Thanks a lot! I didn't know what to think. I had written a whole bunch of stuff that I thought was pretty good, don't you know! You're obviously too tired, mate. These and other less charitable thoughts filled my head.

However, Dave's inherent wisdom was to eventually prove correct. A few years later I did write 'the' song and the change in my ministry happened just as he said.

My two friends saw the desires of their heart for me realised. An infinitely more pleasurable feeling than getting your own way in your own life. As for me, I had the pleasure of experiencing the favour of God in my life without ever having striven for something which I could only receive by grace.

You see, when Isaiah was in the temple and saw the Lord high and lifted up, he was just doing what he and many others before and after him had been called to do. He was worshipping first and foremost. It was God's action to stop him in his tracks and ask the big question, "Who will go for us?" Isaiah's response was still that of a servant, "Here am I, send me."

And what of the song?

CHAPTER 12

The Days of Elijah Story:
Part 2 - Input and Output

As a basis for this part of the story I should at least let you know that, at around the time of writing, neither I nor my church had any ministry which went much further than the four walls of our fellowship. We had made a few tapes, I think we had probably just released the first CD album. It sold a few thousand copies in Ireland alone. Our big neighbour next door, England (where heroes lived!) was quite unchartered territory.

This is how the song came to be composed.

Firstly, the song came from watching television. Not really recommended in Christian songwriting schools, I don't think! It was the end of 1994. I am really fond of television 'review of the year' programmes which normally are aired around late December of each year by the main television networks in Britain and Ireland. I love to watch newsreel and documentary footage of what happened in the year just passed.

1994 was not a great year. You may not recall now, well over a decade later, unless something of that year impacted you personally, so let me remind you what it was like. It was the year of the Rwandan tragedy which claimed one million people's lives. In six weeks an ethnic grouping, roughly the same size as 70% of the entire population of Northern Ireland, were killed in a bloody civil war. The horror was not lost on me living in a country where civil and ethnic strife had been rampant for over 25 years. Indeed, 1994 was also when the first ceasefires in Northern Ireland were declared and when, later, these same ceasefires were broken with acts of atrocious violence.

On the TV review were a lot of daft stories, happy stories, serious stories, and then absolutely devastating stories like the Rwandan situation.

The show is broadcast fairly late in the evening, it isn't really prime time entertainment. All my family had gone to bed and I sat alone and watched the year's story portrayed on the screen from my armchair.

As I watched the review unfold I found myself despairing about the state of the world that God had made and, in prayer, began asking God if He really was in control. How could He be when such terrible things happened? And, anyway, 'Lord, what on Earth sort of days are we living in?'

Now, it's never a great idea to accuse God of not being in control. But it's not a bad idea to ask Him questions when you can. He even says Himself, in Isaiah 1:18, "Come, let us reason together." So, retrospectively, I can excuse my impetuousness by saying that I was reasoning with the Father!

As I sat there and part meditated, part argued and part railed against the unfolding stories that seemed to define a world without hope, that's when I felt in my spirit that He replied to my prayer.

His reply: that, indeed, He was very much in control. These days in which we were living were actually very special times when He would require Christians to be filled with integrity and to stand up for His name. We were to be men and women just like Elijah.

Elijah was a prophet of God who lived in a time when it seemed the majority of people followed a pagan god called Baal. Elijah, in the midst of a lost, wicked and desperate generation, had to challenge the prophets of Baal and all that they believed in. We were to be those who would stand in these days, now, not for our own sake, but for the sake of a world lost and deceived by strange beliefs and strange gods.

If you know the story from 1 Kings 18 you will recall that Elijah was called by God again and again in his ministry to make a stand for His name. In verse 22, Elijah even says, "I am the only prophet of the Lord who is left." Note that his challenge in all that he did was to the people of Israel to come back to their God. They were to turn away from strange and wicked beliefs and practices and return to the Lover of their souls.

Do you ever feel that our world is like that? Do you ever feel that you need to cry out to the nations to return to God?

That's why, for me, I felt I could say, "These are 'Elijah' days."

I also sensed that we needed to be a holy and just people in all our doings and in our witness for Christ. Hence the reference to the 'days of your servant Moses', meaning that righteousness and right living was important in all our attitudes and works. Now, for sure, we are under grace and not under law because of what Christ has done. We are the children of the New Covenant where the demands of the law have been satisfied by His sacrifice. But this righteousness that comes by faith can be no less than the moral law that Moses brought direct from God. It has not been superseded. In fact, you may recall that Jesus reminded us that our righteousness had to exceed that of the Pharisees, who, although misguided, tried to uphold a very high moral code. By God's grace we need to be a holy nation and a royal priesthood.

'Days of great trial, of famine, darkness and sword' is a reflection of the times in which we live when thousands of people still die every day from starvation, malnutrition, disease and war. I recently read that on any one night 1,000 million children go to bed in danger from all these things.

These are the days we live in. We are here for a purpose and for such a time as this. In the midst of all that we see we are called to make a declaration of what and Who we believe in.

The second verse continues with reference to the restoration of unity of the body of Christ. Jesus prayed in John 17 for the unity of His body – "that they may be one even as I and the Father are one..." Ezekiel had a prophetic vision of a valley of dry bones becoming flesh and being knit together. The bones became a mighty army. Whilst the message was initially brought by Ezekiel for the lost hope that Israel felt in their captivity and defeat, it is also widely interpreted as a picture of unity in the Church, and the restoration of hope to a Church under pressure and divided. The reunification of His body.

The restoration of praise and worship to the Church is represented by 'the days of your servant David' in the final portion of the second verse, 'rebuilding a temple of praise'. I've already explained in a previous chapter how it seems that God has determined to restore praise and worship to the lips, and the heart, of His Church. Some folks will ask me about this line and the fact that David didn't actually build the temple. Well, of course, I'm not referring to the grand stone temple that his son Solomon completed, I am talking about, firstly, a 'rebuilding', and secondly, not a temple of stone and timber, but 'a temple of praise'.

David was used by God in his lifetime to introduce praise and thanksgiving with music and song into the tabernacle or temple. The original worship in the tabernacle of Moses did not have the continuous praise and music and song around the Ark that rose up in David's day. Rather, only one man could minister before the holy place where the Ark was located. Nor was there any music in that place, only the sound of little golden bells which were sewn around the bottom of the high priest's robe to let the other priests outside the most holy place know that he was still moving around!

David, however, built a little tent or house over and around the Ark of the Covenant and established a pattern of continuous praise in that place. You will find reference to this restoration of David's tabernacle in Amos 9:11, "In that day I will restore David's fallen tent." Whilst commentators see in this verse a reference to the restoration of Israel and, as unfolded in the New Testament, the unity of the Church, many see the reference in the context of the prophetic book as referring in some part to the restoration of true praise and worship in the body.

Finally, the line with the phrase 'days of the harvest' points toward what is the ultimate call and purpose for the Christian, to go into all the world and make disciples of all nations.

When I was growing up in Belfast, I was sent out to a local Brethren Gospel Hall for the midweek children's meeting. Some of the great Bible teaching on types of Christ and patterns of things to come which are embodied in the teachings of the Old Testament obviously rubbed off on me.

That I could refer to these Old Testament stories to present the reality of the hope found in Jesus Christ for the world was not open to question in my mind. This is known as 'typology' in theological circles. That's why I never wrote that these were like days of Elijah, or like days of Moses; I chose to use the word 'are' as a reference to the constancy and consistency of our God, the same yesterday, today and forever.

The overall theme of the song is hope, a hope that is secure in the knowledge that God's hands are on our lives and His creation. The themes of the verses – declaration, righteousness, unity and worship, I chose to express by reference to the characters that represented these virtues in the Old Testament. It is, in essence, a song of hope for the Church and the world in times of great trial.

The chorus is, I suppose, the ultimate declaration of hope.

Christ's return.

The chorus is paraphrased from the books of Revelation and Daniel and the vision that was seen of the coming King, referring to the return of Christ and the year of Jubilee. Theologians and Bible commentators believe that Israel probably never properly celebrated this particular 50th year Jubilee, and that it will only be truly celebrated when the Messiah, Christ, returns.

That, no doubt, is true, but I reckon that a Jubilee is also an apt description of what happens when Christ comes into anyone's life at any time for debts are cancelled and a captive is set free. Indeed, Christ read from Isaiah 61 when He was in the temple and declared that this 'Jubilee' passage was fulfilled in Him. Yet another Old Testament theme made complete in Christ.

All of these thoughts were in my head when I came to church early one Sunday in 1995. It was only a stream of thoughts and statements and not, by any means, a complete worship song. I recall having some sort of tune and musing over the words, but that's about it.

We have two services and Paul Reid, the pastor of my home church, spoke during the first service on the 'valley of dry bones' from Ezekiel 37. I took a prompt from this and, in the thirty minutes between the services, wrote down the words and chords in the kitchen of our church building, teaching it to my band as I went. We sang it at the end of the second service. It was a song birthed out of a personal experience and an encounter with God and finalised within a corporate gathering of God's people. It was a song using imagery not perhaps common to the typical worship song lyrics, but it was a song from my heart.

How do you express the sense that these might be days, not of failure and submission, but of the sort of resilient, declaring, even arrogant trust and hope that Elijah had in his God? That these are not days of God stepping back and allowing the world and the Church to roll uncontrolled towards eternity, but rather days when He is calling on His body to make a stand, to offer right praises and to declare that He is totally in control. Well, I reckon you may write the words, 'These are the days of Elijah' and 'These are the days of David'. I've used word pictures and biblical characters to make that expression, but this is no different from many of the great hymn writers and even King David himself.

I presented the song to the church that day with a short word of explanation, and we sang it as our worship.

Now the rest, I suppose, is history. There is no mechanism within the church, (conspiracy theorists take note!), for making people sing a particular song, or for increasing its use in the national or international Church body. As far as I was concerned the song was for our congregation, on that day and at that time. On many other occasions we have sung a song together in our church which has disappeared without trace after one rendition. I had no indication that this song would be any different.

However, God obviously had other ideas and it is now sung almost all over the world, despite its apparent complexity and obscure lyrics! Grammatically, there may be the odd aberration, but thankfully the Church has forgiven me that particular shortcoming. The imagery may be a little deeper than some others would prefer, but it reflected my heart's cry at that time.

I must make it clear that I did not set out to write an overly complex or 'secret' song, and I hope the testimony above bears that out.

There is a postscript to this story for those who believe the song means something entirely different. In 1999 I was privileged to be in Israel at Yom Kippur for a celebration with hundreds of Messianic Jews. A very kind, gentle and humorous Messianic brother had a bit of fun arguing with me that I, as an Irish Christian, could never have written a song which explores some of the themes that many, (non-replacement theology here!) Jewish believers believe are the themes and indications of Christ's return:

1. The Spirit and Power of Elijah in the Church.
2. The restoration of Israel to righteousness in Christ.
3. The restoration of praise and worship and the unity of the body particularly with a renewed and redeemed Israel under Christ.

The Messianic believers sing the song with great gusto and this alternative biblical interpretation. A fine evangelist and teacher, David Reagan, has written and produced a CD sermon on a Messianic interpretation of the song which explains that particular theology beautifully.

For me, I only know what I wrote.

I felt prompted by the Holy Spirit and put down those thoughts which I believe He placed in me. Perhaps it was His desire to say something more than I personally intended and to do more with this song than I first considered. But isn't that the way worship is? You come with your offering, seeking only to bless the One to whom you give it, and He, in His great mercy, uses it in a way you never even imagined.

All of these restored things like justice, righteousness, integrity, unity, praise and worship and revival are considered by many to be a herald of the last days and Christ's return. Personally, I don't know – I believe I wrote what God was telling me to write and He seems to have used the song in many ways for many people. For me, it expressed hope and certainty at a time in the world's history which for many spoke only of despair and uncertainty.

It is unusual, for sure, and I am not encouraging you to go away and dig the most obscure theological thoughts out of your head in order to emulate some sort of a pattern. I have written many much simpler songs with much less words!

No, I just want to raise the point that technical ability, skill, poetry, melody, dedication, the words, craft, structure . . . all the things we know we must address are all very well. You will write a very fine song using all those skills. Our popular music charts are filled with songs written by folks gifted in many of these areas. But in the absence of 'offering', 'sacrifice', 'inspiration', and 'revelation' they will mean little; whilst the grammatically clumsy, awkward, poorly-paced song can soar to the heights of heaven, if a worshiping heart is behind it. I know beyond a shadow of a doubt that many of my songwriting colleagues can tell similar and even more intriguing stories of how God uses the unusual and seemingly inappropriate to work out His purposes in worship.

And here's the last point. The real test of any hymn or praise and worship song, I feel, is that it is sung gladly by people! That's when you know you have mined a rich seam of creativity that when God's people sing, they are able to join their hearts with the writer and identify with the song; to give Him praise! Even if the meaning is a bit unusual.

So be a worshipper first, have a servant heart second, and be a songwriter last of all.

Days of Elijah

These are the days of Elijah,
Declaring the word of the Lord:
And these are the days of Your servant, Moses,
Righteousness being restored.
And though these are days of great trial,
Of famine and darkness and sword,
Still, we are the voice in the desert crying,
"Prepare ye the way of the Lord."

Behold He comes riding on the clouds,
Shining like the sun at the trumpet call;
Lift your voice, it's the year of Jubilee,
And out of Zion's hill salvation comes.

And these are the days of Ezekiel,
The dry bones becoming as flesh;
And these are the days of Your servant David,
Rebuilding a temple of praise.
And these are the days of the harvest,
O the fields are as white in Your world,
And we are the labourers in Your vineyard,
Declaring the word of the Lord.

CHAPTER 13

Those Whom God Calls:
Nine to Five or 24/7?

Inspired?

I hope so!

Are these WARRIOR POETS only those gifted in the area of music and creative arts? Are they only songwriters?

Not at all. If the story of Barak and the 'wrong guys' from Naphtali and Zebulun teach us anything, it is the reality of being willing, in whatever sphere of life we find ourselves, to be worshippers in spirit and truth to the Father.

We haven't mentioned much on possibly the greatest WARRIOR POET of all until now – the shepherd king, David, the man after God's own heart and the Sweet Psalmist of Israel.

Those of you brought up in the theology of typology which I touched on a little in the last few chapters will know that David is seen as a forerunning type of Christ. A shepherd, a warrior and a king. The one who at the end of his reign over the nation of Israel, when his son Solomon took the throne, had bequeathed all the prosperity and safety we looked at in chapter 5.

There is a lot one could learn about worship from this one man, his escapades, adventures and life and the Psalms that he and his co-worshippers composed and recorded have been the subject of entire books. Just one of those compositions, Psalm 23, has had such an impact on the history of literature, poetry and theology that writers have devoted entire volumes to an exposition of this one song.

But I want to focus on just one event in the life he lived to hopefully encourage you in worship even more, whoever you are.

In and around the books of 2nd Samuel or 1st Chronicles we read the story of the Ark of the Covenant's return to Jerusalem, the City of David, and how King David pitched a tent for the Ark to construct what became known as 'David's tabernacle'. You find that story in 1 Chronicles 15 or 2 Samuel 6.

The Ark contained the tablets of stone upon which God wrote the Ten Commandments, some manna and Aaron's rod that budded.

God's glory dwelt over the Ark and it was first placed, hundreds of years before, in the Holy of Holies in Moses' tabernacle where it was accessible only to the high priest, once each year, to make atonement for the sins of the people of Israel. The story of the Ark and the imagery incorporated in its design and location in the Mosaic tabernacle is fascinating (Exodus 35-38), particularly in reference to what Christ has done, but we want to consider some thoughts on worship lifestyle and relevance based on David's tabernacle in Chronicles.

Once David brings the Ark back to Jerusalem he places it on Mount Zion and then erects a tent over it. Some commentators suggest it may have resembled a small clay or timber structure, others regard it as a small tabernacle or tent. Whatever its structure, David understood it as the 'dwelling place' of his God.

Interestingly, there was already a full Mosaic tabernacle, (that is, after the design and instructions God gave to Moses), not that far away at Gibeon at that time which, obviously, was missing an Ark. But David doesn't take the Ark to what you would think would be its proper location. He prefers to place it in Jerusalem and in a flimsy, easily accessible structure.

Through the centuries theologians have tried to explain his actions. It looks on face value that David is breaking the rules or somehow using his kingship and position to, at least, bend them a little. There's possibly some truth in this because of the Jewish tradition of the ongoing revelation of the Scriptures and the ability of the high priest to review God's actions in light of Scripture interpretation. It may be that David regarded himself as, essentially, a priest ministering to God even though he was not of that tradition.

However, I think the best explanations seem to come from those that see this event as a reflection and foretaste of Christ's work through the Cross, at a point many years into the future.

David has placed the evidence of God's presence, not in the most holy place of the tabernacle, hidden away from all but one man, but under the king's authority and possession and visible and accessible to many.

All the accessibility and formality of the original tabernacle of Moses are changed and so it is as if David has represented a reflection of what God will do in Christ in making access to Him open to many.

Some theologians regard this change as evidence of a Davidic Covenant where David is modelling out the change in the accessibility into God's presence which will mark what Christ will do. All of the original Mosaic sacrifices and offerings are there, but now they're accompanied by other acts of worship and praise involving singing and the playing of musical instruments.

David even carries out some of the functions of the high priest from Moses' days, another picture or reflection of Christ's work and the accessibility of a kingly man into the holy place.

We also get a glimpse of the fulltime 'employees', mostly it seems from the Levitical Priesthood, who were to be the permanent worshippers at and around the Ark of the Covenant, regularly, daytime and evening, and probably continuously day after day. The lead priest is there, but so are many other priests and associates worshipping around God's presence over the Ark.

So it is from this passage that many draw their inspiration and authority for the role of worship leaders in the Church, as perhaps separate or different from pastors and ministers. It also is used to explain why worship leading might be deemed an appropriate employment in the Church.

It saddens me when theologians vent their dissatisfaction with the role of worship leader, (or as Matt Redman would say – Lead Worshipper), in the modern Church. One quote of a well-respected author and academic is, "The notion of a 'worship leader' ... is so bizarre." Unusual and uncompromising language there! Others point to the lack of theological education as evidence of why some worship leaders should never be let loose in the congregational environment.

But, hey! worry not. They probably said much the same things about the shepherd king of Israel when he placed the Ark in Jerusalem and pitched the tent over it.

Throughout this book I hope I have stressed how worship should be seen to be not just one form or style or action but part of every act of life that we commit. Somewhere along the line of Church history there seems to have been a mind shift in popular culture that has us all convinced that unless you're a fulltime musician or worship pastor somehow you're not quite making the grade.

When David made the Ark of the Covenant accessible to all, so accessible that even the sparrow and the swallow came and nested at the altar, then it opened the way for all to come and worship in God's presence. There was still a high priest, but access to the Ark, access to the presence of God Himself was open and visible to all. Whoever or whatever could come and worship.

This makes perfect sense, doesn't it? For as we said right at the beginning of this book, this was what you and I were made for. Everyone is a worshipper.

David did choose men of skill to lead the praises, and they chose understudies to assist them (see 1 Chronicles 15). But even then, there were a few interesting choices.

One that stands out for me is Asaph. We mentioned him in the last chapter, very briefly. In case you've forgotten, Asaph is the writer of Psalm 73. A beautifully worded reflection on life, the world, prosperity, why the wicked do well whilst the righteous suffer and then the wisdom and revelation of the sanctuary of God. What skills did the man who penned such a beautiful poem have?

What skills indeed? Well in 1 Chronicles 15:19 we learn that Asaph was, firstly, selected as a musician whose job was to sound the brass cymbals. Asaph was a cymbal crasher. Has anyone ever led worship in your church with cymbals lately? No? I'm not surprised. It would be an interesting, if nerve jangling, experience I'm sure, but I'm pretty certain there would be some interesting reactions from the members.

Hundreds of years after this time when Asaph was chosen to begin his musical career as the one who bangs the cymbals, he gets a mention in the book of Nehemiah. After the rebuilding of the walls of Jerusalem, the book of the Law is found in the ruins and Ezra the priest is required to read it. Nehemiah learns about how worship was such an important part of the Davidic worship era and learns something else. In Nehemiah 12:46 Nehemiah says, with some poignancy it would appear, that "long ago in the days of David and Asaph there were directors for the choirs and music."

Asaph, the cymbal crasher, is mentioned in partnership with and alongside the Psalmist and King of Israel, David. His fame was such that the humble percussionist stands shoulder to shoulder with his king as one of God's great earthly worship leaders. This is just another sign of the work that God can do with whatever skill we have, if we apply that skill to worshipping His name.

So, really, it is not just about musicians and worship leaders and artists. It's about everyone.

I've been a worship leader in my home church in Belfast for around 20 years now. That's a very long time, I think. I have a team of faithful and unendingly patient musicians who support me at home and abroad. They told me I have to mention them by name in this book ... Andrew, Karen, Brian, Robert, Gary, Kathy, Michelle, Alison, Anna and Maggie, many thanks!

But before that, I was a worship leader in a small house fellowship of around fourteen people for 3 or 4 years before joining the larger congregation where I now serve. Around 17 years ago when I was just over 30 years old, God led me to a decision which was to change my life.

No, it wasn't into fulltime music ministry, nor to the signing of a record deal with a major distributor nor anything one could consider as remotely 'churchy' or music ministry oriented. It was to start a business as a self-employed noise and acoustic consultant.

I felt as strong a call as I had ever had that this was what God wanted me to do. I gave up my salaried post as a college teacher and, with a wife and child, an overdraft, some borrowed cash, actually from my pastor, Paul Reid, it was his holiday money – and, yes, despite what he might say, I did give it all back … eventually, and a tiny little start-up grant from a local enterprise organisation, I launched myself upon an unsuspecting noisy world!

F R Mark and Associates, Noise and Acoustic Consultants, was born. I rented an office for £10 per week (about $18) in a town outside Belfast, bought an Amstrad PC computer and a telephone and went for it.

Now, was this call any less in God's eyes than a call to fulltime worship ministry? Was the Father's hand set more lightly upon this venture than it would upon a church-based career? Was this just a passing diversion before God really blessed me with enough royalty income to spend glorious day after day reclining on a leather sofa in the music room, creating heavenly melodies in splendid isolation from the rotten old world?

Actually … no.

In our society we separate the sacred and the secular as if one had a higher calling than the other. It was never so in the Hebrew mindset. The Apostle Paul went out of his way to talk about all the different parts of the body and how one part should not think itself more superior than another. Whatever our hand finds to do we should do it with all our might, as on to the Lord. In other words, your work can be an act of worship just as distinctive and important as the finest song that will ever be written.

Maybe you can remember the verses right in the middle of Genesis 4 where God mentions Jabal, Jubal and Tubal-Cain as the respective fathers of all the artists, all the manual workers and all the farmers. We noted then that it was as if in the midst of this passage relating to God's pursuit of a worshipping heart, He reminds us that everyone's life and work is to be offered as an act of worship.

Wouldn't it be interesting if when we get to heaven and are queuing up for the various precious stones and other shiny rewards for our service, if we spotted a chartered accountant, a home help, and a farmer in the line ahead of us. Maybe God will tell them,

"Well done, good and faithful servant," and remind them of the staggering act of worship that they made to Him.

"Hold on, Lord," I might protest, "these guys never wrote a single, decent, worship song between them!"

And then, maybe, He might remind them, and me, of the time when the accountant convinced the businessman to be honest in his dealings with the Inland Revenue, and saved him from great disgrace; when the home help spent longer than the minimum wage salary time allocated to make sure the ageing widower adequately finished his lunch; when the farmer rose early day after day to nurture and generate food for the countless thousands of supermarket shoppers who knew nothing of his labour. Maybe I'd feel a bit guilty!

You see, here's the amazing thing! In the fulness of time God has blessed some of the songs of worship that I have composed and I now receive some financial reward for this creativity. I am truly blessed and thankful for His grace in this area. But more than that, being self-employed meant I was able to go to conferences, concert tours, visit churches all over the world and fund some of my early recordings, without needing to ask my employer for days off, unless I was talking to myself at the time! Having that income meant I didn't have to strain to produce another song, trying desperately to maintain my highest motivation, whilst all the while knowing that I needed the income from the song to survive.

Now, don't get me wrong. I truly admire the fulltime worship leaders and musicians that have blessed us all over the years. Men like Noel Richards who have mortgaged homes and sacrificed income to bring God's people together in worship. Men and women like Chris Bowater, Trish Morgan and Dave Billborough who ministered so graciously in the early years of the worship renewal, visiting Northern Ireland from England, for little more than travel expenses and a kind word. Men and women of faith who heard the call to step out into fulltime worship ministry when there wasn't any real support or assistance, or when the Christian Copyright Licensing International organisation had not yet been conceived.

But one thing is sure. If you ask these guys what motivated their decision they will surely tell you that it wasn't the need for success, or the desire to be in 'fulltime service', (we're all in fulltime service, by the way), or money, or recognition, or even just the kudos that comes with being part of the music business. No, not at all. It was God's call. No different from my call to business. Just the same call as the shop worker, the taxi driver, the business manager, the nurse, or the doctor. Just the same call as all of our calls into the area that God wants us to be in. To be true worshippers with what Paul called our acceptable sacrifice, even our very lives.

God has to be careful with us. I know now, in retrospect, that He needed to slow me down and rein me in. My natural attitude would be to run before I could walk. That if an opportunity for some 'fulltime worship leader' role had been presented to me, I would have got totally caught up in something that wasn't for me and blown everything. He knew that I needed to be a noise consultant. (Honest!) He also knew that Matt Redman, Chris Tomlin and other fulltime leaders would be good stewards of the ministry that they are now in. He knew that they would have to face trials and troubles and be overcomers so that He could express His worship and touch millions of Christians around the world through them. He knows what each of us need to be and where we need to be.

So, here's the thing. Don't strive to be in what is known as 'worship ministry' or some related 'fulltime ministry' and don't exclude your contribution because you're not in some of those ministries. These are callings that demand great sacrifice and great commitment. Don't strive to become a 'fulltime musician' because it seems the appropriate thing to do and is pretty cool, actually! For sure, if the call on your life seems so strong and real, then if the door opens, go for it. But don't expect it to be any different than any other work. There are great disappointments and challenges on that walk.

Whatever you will do, it has to be a call. It must be a call. And it can be a call to work in a supermarket to feed your family, and play your songs of worship in your spare time. That's as high a call as anyone, if it's what God calls you to do.

And what of my business? Well, God has truly blessed, because like everything we have, it was never really 'my' business. It was another opportunity to do something, with all my might, as an offering to Him. I have since sold and passed on that business to the guys that used to work for me. They have clients across the whole spectrum of business life in Ireland, including pub and club owners, entertainment companies, government and industry. I have met hundreds and thousands of ordinary people that I otherwise would never have known. Some of my songs have been motivated and formed around these relationships. I earned some money! I was able to give employment to three fulltime employees and a couple of part-timers. I now have been graced to take on the role of Director of Worship in CFC, my home church, and work a few days a week doing it. My songs have gone from Belfast to all over the world. God's call was a good one!

I am still not in fulltime ministry. I call into the acoustics business about once a week. I work in the church another two and I still teach in the local University in the Architecture Department. Maybe one day soon I'll hear the call to go fulltime. Maybe the other businesses will decline! Maybe I'll need to find work elsewhere. Maybe I'll never hear the 'fulltime ministry' call. All I know is, and all I would share is, this:

Everyone is called to worship Him with their whole heart and life, in spirit and in truth. His ways and His thoughts are higher than ours, that He knows the plans that He has for us, and that He knows the way we are to take. Listen for the call, and no matter how strange it might seem, go where He calls you to go.

Perhaps it comes down to this. Work the nine to five, but worship 24/7!

CHAPTER 14

What If Worship . . .?

We're not far from the end of the book now. I hope at least some of it has made sense and that you've been challenged.

The Christian life and walk has been the subject of many books. Discipleship is a subject that is presented again and again to try and give us some clarity of understanding regarding our walk through life. And it's not surprising really.

Those of you that have been Christians for some time, let's do a little exercise. Think back to when you were around 16 or 18 years old and the Christian or church-based friends that you had then. How many of them are still walking the walk? How many are still committed to the cause of Christ and take an active part in the Church today? If you are in your late thirties or forties now, it's entirely probable that very few of those previously fired up and enthusiastic believers are still carrying on. The probability is that most of them will have taken something of a back seat in life and, whilst ticking the Christian box in a survey or census about religious beliefs, will no longer be active in the Church.

And those of you young in the faith who are reading this book. The sad fact is that, unless something radically changes, many of your friends and fellow believers over the next few years will cease to be active and fervent for their Lord but rather settle for the nominal Christian life of attending church on a Sunday and generally forgetting about God for the rest of the week.

Hence the great array of lifestyle and '10 step program' books out there to encourage the Christian to keep running the race and to keep us going.

But here's a novel thought.

What if it was just all about worship? What if worship pervaded everything we did in life? What if we just had to shift our understanding of every activity that we embarked upon to understand this one simple fact that, whatever we did, it was all about worship? That by maintaining our worshipping heart we would increase rather than decrease in our walk with God.

Let me give you a slightly risky example, for which I hope I don't receive any letters of complaint.

You know how it is possible to read the Scriptures and determine that God wants to bless you, right? You know how it's easy to see that if you give to God, then He gives back a full measure with, as the Bible says, it all pushed down and running over? Good.

Well, unfortunately, some parts of the Church have taken this and turned it into a technique, or method, for receiving blessing. You know the thing.

"If you're out there reading this book, and God has placed upon your heart a desire to bless this ministry, then I urge you to respond to that desire and send 100 dollars (or pounds) to this address. I guarantee that you will receive a blessing that is ten times, at least, what you will send and God will bless you with abundance. Aaaymen!"

I'm joking, by the way.

What's wrong with a statement like that? Actually, not a great deal in essence, but an awful lot in practice. What has been done is that one of the truths of God's blessing, provision and response to worship has been turned into a formulaic 'get rich quick' pitch. At the risk of being boring, the heart behind the statement is all wrong. The heart of worship gives to God, expecting nothing in return, because it has been exposed to the beauty and majesty and glory of the One who is pre-eminent and who deserves all our worship. Who cares, faced with that splendour, whether He might bless you or not? However, God in His graciousness and mercy will indeed pour out His blessing, as He sees fit, on that worshipping heart.

What man has done here is almost hijack God's worship to gain financially. Instead of concentrating on the offering, and the heart that wants to give and give again, the concentration is moved to the potential for reward.

A simple, but an entirely dangerous, difference.

And, perhaps, it is the same in other areas of the Christian walk. What about prayer? I know one great local preacher here in Belfast who regularly tells his congregation that he has never asked God for anything for himself since his conversion. You see, he simply trusts and understands that God knows what he needs and will surely provide. He does, of course, pray long and fervently for his church, for others, for the land and for the purpose of getting to know more of his God in his daily walk. God has blessed his ministry greatly. His prayer is much closer to worship than simply a 'bless me please' request list.

What about the poor, the lost, the hopeless? What about justice, righteousness, and mercy or the increasing breakdown of our society? Can worship have any impact on these areas of our lives?

Growing up in Belfast from the late 1960s to the 1990s, we had an acute sense of the complex issues that form around the issues of 'justice' and 'mercy'. Justice is sometimes defined as 'getting what you deserve' and requires the impartation of great wisdom in the decision making. Mercy can also be defined as 'not getting what you deserve' and, perhaps, requires even greater wisdom.

Christians in Northern Ireland found themselves torn between rationalising the injustices of past generations to sections of the community and coping with the 'now' injustice of terrorism unleashed on the innocents in the society in which they lived. Trying to maintain a righteous perspective takes great searching of your heart in circumstances like that. And, of course, if the heart is where your worship is born and generated, then the twin themes of worship and justice go hand in hand.

Indeed, worship can be twinned with many themes in the Christian experience. I hope I have shown throughout this book that worship seems to be at the very core of all our transformed lives and all aspects of it. Justice, the poor, evangelism, all these facets are intrinsically linked to the worshipping heart.

Is it possible that God knows that a worshipping heart, fulfilling the very purpose for which it was created, is a heart that will naturally be drawn to do justice and righteousness? Is it possible that Jesus understood and expressed the Father's heart because He lived a worshipping lifestyle to the Father?

Consider these words in John 17:4, "I brought glory to you here on earth by doing everything that you told me to do." Jesus' acts of obedience are equivalent to Him giving His Father glory or, in other words, to Him engaging in worship.

There is a current theme being expressed, mainly with some justification, that our worship has become so experiential, so 'me', so 'encounter based' and 'intimate', that we are spending all our time in what we think is 'worship' and doing nothing for the rest of the world. This is an understandable perspective.

We like to sing about giving God the glory. What if, like Jesus, it was our obedience to His commands that gave Him glory? We are then encouraged to give our songs relevance to society by incorporating more lyrical reference to culture, oppression, sin, hunger and many of the ills that beset our world so that the worshipper's heart and mind can be educated on what we need to do. But, is there not a problem with this?

If this were the case, then might there not be a correlation between the lack of a mission heart, or social action, or reaching out to the poor and disadvantaged in society and the churches that have embraced contemporary worship? If it were true that the upsurge of modern worship deflected the Christian from these areas of service, then should we therefore expect the churches which have adopted a more recent hymnody to have a lesser world perspective?

Yet, by and large, the opposite seems to be true. Church congregations such as Soul Survivor, Ichthus, Vineyard, and Church of Christ the King, and others from all the traditional denominations which have espoused and absorbed new forms of worship have found themselves at the forefront of social action, increasing their response to mission and reaching out to the community, often with the 'new' sung worship as part of that advance.

When I was a young churchgoer and the subject of worship came up, the most memorable and repeated phrase that I can recall was this: "You can worship God in washing the dishes just as much as singing a song."

I never could quite get my head round that. Firstly, I hate washing dishes! I can still recall the absolute unbridled joy when my wife and I finally saved enough money to buy and install an automatic dishwasher. The person that invented the automatic dishwasher should be elevated to sainthood, in my opinion. So now that I simply open the door, shove all the dinner dishes into whatever space is left and press the button, has this mechanical marvel robbed me of an opportunity for a meaningful act of worship?

No, of course not. In fact, I generally utter a little song of praise as that button is pressed.

This innocent enough statement is, once again, focusing on the practice rather than the lover's heart that underscores every act of worship.

We looked at one of the first acts of worship in the story of Cain and Abel in Genesis 4. That act was an offering to God.

Offering is a good definition of worship. Bringing something of yourself, whether it's a possession or an action, and giving it over to God is a profound act of worship and 'offering' may be one of the simplest and finest definitions of what worship is.

As Paul Baloche writes:

I bring an offering of worship to my King,
No one on earth deserves the praises that I bring;
Jesus, may You receive the honour that You're due.
O Lord, I bring an offering to You.
(Offering, P Baloche, Integrity Music 2003)

When we offered our lives to Jesus in the first place, it was a key act of worship. It was the end of God's pursuit of us, and the beginning of our pursuit of God. Well, a life that began with worship should, of course, continue in worship, and the other facets of the Christian life and even the actions that we carry out, should also proceed from worship.

CHAPTER 15

Worship and Evangelism

This chapter is not particularly long. That's not because it's not important. On the contrary, one of the greatest mysteries of God's work through the Holy Spirit on this earth is how, in the midst of worship, with rarely a spoken word or explanation of the five spiritual laws, people can be drawn to the saving grace of Christ.

The only reason that this is a short chapter is because there is a wonderful text by Sally Morgenthaller called Worship Evangelism which investigates and explains this dynamic better than I ever can.

The concept of worship having a role in evangelism impacted me one November night in 1995 in Belfast.

Two good friends of mine had decided that it was time that a 'Robin Mark' worship concert was organised in the city, not in a church, but in one of the larger venues in Belfast. Even the phrase 'worship concert' seemed to me to be something of an oxymoron. How can worship be a concert, and how could a concert really involve worship? Would there not be a conflict between the ideas of performance and audience and participation and leadership and congregation and individuals? My head could not figure it out.

I never did figure it out, actually. At least, not until after the event.

On the day of the show a full house of ticket-buying concert goers squeezed into one of Belfast's main halls and my band and I took the stage. We began with a few performance type songs, a few humorous sing-a-longs with, I reckoned, the intention to make people as relaxed as possible. I'd only ever led worship in my church, I really had no idea how to transfer that to a concert event.

There had been other events in the city involving artists and musicians from different parts of the world over a number of years, but these were essentially structured and presented either to bless the body of Christ, or had a distinct evangelistic context, with songs to match.

This was something different.

We had an interval, as you do in Christian events, and came back for the second set afterwards. The second half was straight, full-on worship music. No apologies, no explanation, just a continuous time of worship with the crowd. Now, in the context of the USA, or even England at that time, this was nothing particularly radical. In relation to today, we have become comfortable and used to the concept. But back in Belfast in 1995, I assure you, it was pretty new.

We had a good night, people left happy and built up, and then through the two promoters we received the news. In total 8 people had given their lives to Christ at the concert or shortly afterwards, because of that night.

No appeal had been presented, no invitation made, no clear presentation of the gospel message had been possible. We had just joined together to engage with God in worship.

The same impact repeated itself concert after concert, usually through stories passed back to us from those that would attend. One of the stewards at another of our Belfast concerts a few years later was escorting some folks from the car park and happened to ask if they had enjoyed the night. In the course of the ensuing conversation a young man who had been invited to the time of worship, and had been touched during the evening, gave his life to the Lord.

What was going on here? For sure, folks had invited friends and loved ones who were not Christians to come, and had probably by their lifestyles, actions and words modelled out the gospel message again and again. But what was it about a night of worship music that brought the final revelation to those lost hearts?

It was, I would suggest, the very presence of Christ in the worship.

The Bible says that God inhabits the praises of His people,

and Jesus did tell us that if He was lifted up that He would draw all men to Him. We know that this phrase was mainly in regard to the Cross, but there is no doubt that when the name of Jesus is exalted in praise, people will be drawn to Him.

I did a seminar a few years back and a young intern asked this very question.

"How can worship draw people to Christ, unless the songs have a specific lyric based evangelistic content that is designed to draw the person in?"

It was a very good question and one that begs a good answer. If the songs are not, as some say, horizontal and directed to our audience or congregation rather than vertical and directed to God, how is it possible to impact non-Christians? For me, the best place to find a Scriptural answer to that question is in the Song of Solomon.

In the first portion of this Scripture we have the enquiry of the searching heart. Or, if you like, the very question that a world confused by many religions, deities and apparently spiritual movements might well ask.

Friends:

"How is your beloved better than others, most beautiful of women? How is your beloved better than others, that you charge us so?" (Song of Solomon 5:9)

How is our God better than any other god? The Beloved had asked her friends to help them search for her lover. She had presented the need for her friends to search after and find the one she loved. Her friends then asked the obvious question, "Why, what's so special about him?"

The Beloved then answers this question in a lavish description of her lover, which uses the language of worship all the way through. Phrases which you will know, "He is Altogether Lovely", the "Fairest of Ten Thousand", and "This is my Friend", are laced throughout this description. These are words of worship which, even today, we have placed in our worship songs and sing to our Beloved.

176

Beloved:

My lover is radiant and ruddy, outstanding among ten thousand. His head is purest gold; his hair is wavy and black as a raven. His eyes are like doves by the water streams, washed in milk, mounted like jewels. His cheeks are like beds of spice yielding perfume. His lips are like lilies dripping with myrrh. His arms are rods of gold set with chrysolite. His body is like polished ivory decorated with sapphires. His legs are pillars of marble set on bases of pure gold. His appearance is like Lebanon, choice as its cedars. His mouth is sweetness itself; he is altogether lovely. This is my lover, this my friend, O daughters of Jerusalem. (Song of Solomon 5:10-16)

And what is the reaction of the friends to this portion of lavish praise, this outward verbal show of love and affection, this act of worship?

Friends:

Where has your lover gone, most beautiful of women? Which way did your lover turn, that we may look for him with you? (Song of Solomon 6:1)

The worshipping beloved one, giving worship to her Lover, has caused the hearts of those gathered around to seek after and find the Lover for themselves.

It is a beautiful picture but it reveals a solid truth. Whatever we do as an act of worship, be it songs, service, work, sacrifice, if it is done for and to the Lover of our souls, then those that are around us at that time cannot help but be drawn to Him as well. Worship is evangelism.

CHAPTER 16
Worship and the Poor

The magazine article was the transcript of an interview with a well-known praise leader and musician. Although he had led worship at major events in the UK for many years he was just getting ready to embark on a new adventure to the mission field and aid provision overseas. When asked why he was making this radical decision to step back from the limelight, so to speak, his reply read something like this:

"I think for too long the Church has been enjoying itself and being blessed singing songs and having a great time, but it's about time that we turned our focus off ourselves and out to a needy world."

I understand this sentiment, I think; but, on the other hand, there is something that doesn't quite ring true about the response. I hope I have managed to convince you in the thoughts shared in this book so far, that, if nothing else, singing songs and having a good time is not what defines 'worship'. I think it defines 'partying' and whilst 'partying' can and is a part of 'worshipping' as well as being a fun thing to do, it is only another outward expression of something much deeper.

Remember, the Bible makes it clear that whatever means we use to express our worship, it is the heart behind the expression that establishes the worth, or otherwise, of the offering.

That one would perceive worship and helping the poor as two unrelated things can't be correct, can it? Should there not be some dynamic connection between these two activities? They are, for sure, both acts of service.

I am indebted again to two very fine Ulstermen of my acquaintance. One, Johnny Park, worship leader and youth minister, and the other, writer, broadcaster, and Presbyterian minister, Steve Stockman.

When Johnny was releasing one of his excellent recordings a few years back in our church with a special concert night, he tied up with Steve to highlight the need for Christians to take our responsibility to the poor and dispossessed of this world. The launch of the worship CD was related to lifestyle choices, a need to provide financial support for the sick and the hurting of this earth, and a call to remember our brothers and sisters burdened and ensnared in abject poverty.

This is a call that has been echoed down through the centuries and to which the Christian Church, with the message of the gospel that seeks to free the oppressed, feed the hungry and rescue and release those in chains, has readily answered.

In the course of the concert Johnny sang and led us in worship, and Stephen presented the need for ministry to the disadvantaged of this world; all in balance and equilibrium as two related activities.

I was most inspired, that night. In fact, I had written the prelude to the song Come Heal This Land based on the thoughts expressed.

> Let the exile come,
> Let the stranger come,
> Let the weary come find rest.
> All you homeless sons,
> All you widowed ones,
> Call the poor and the dispossessed.
>
> For a table waits, in your Father's house,
> Where the hungry come and eat;
> And there's a place of rest,
> At your Father's breast,
> Where His mercy is complete.
> (Robin Mark, Integrity Music, 2002)

What is the connection between acts of worship and the poor? We could draw a number of thoughts on this theme.

We could highlight how the mass of African American slaves

drew inspiration from the gospel to worship with songs of hope for a better day to come, that would be a connection. We could relate the story of the one-time slave trader John Newton, saved by amazing grace and turning his back on that trade to write songs and lead many to lives of worship. We could note the great songs of gospel liberation and freedom that flowed from the lips and instruments of the Salvationists in Victorian England as they trudged the streets, blessing the poor, bringing release to captives and feeding the hungry.

Yes, worship and social action are not unrelated.

But what does the Bible say about the need for us to be worshippers and the need to care for the lost of this world?

Well, it says many things in many places, but we will look at just two portions of Scripture that, hopefully, will inspire us to worship and, thereby, to reach out to the poor; for the two, in the context of what is real worship, go hand in hand.

Firstly, that worship leader chap at the beginning of the chapter did have some measure of a point, actually, about the songs. Once again it's an issue of the heart, but let's look at Isaiah 1:11-17,

"The multitude of your sacrifices – what are they to me?" says the LORD. I have more than enough of burnt offerings, of rams and the fat of fattened animals; I have no pleasure in the blood of bulls and lambs and goats. When you come to appear before me, who has asked this of you, this trampling of my courts? Stop bringing meaningless offerings! Your incense is detestable to me. New Moons, Sabbaths and convocations—I cannot bear your evil assemblies. Your New Moon festivals and your appointed feasts my soul hates. They have become a burden to me; I am weary of bearing them. When you spread out your hands in prayer, I will hide my eyes from you; even if you offer many prayers, I will not listen. Your hands are full of blood; wash and make yourselves clean.

Take your evil deeds out of my sight! Stop doing wrong, learn to do right! Seek justice, encourage the oppressed. Defend the cause of the fatherless, plead the case of the widow."

In this passage, God expresses His intolerance of empty worship – of getting together, having our feasts and celebrations, even praying our prayers when they are empty. "Learn to do right," He cries, "Seek justice, encourage the oppressed, defend the cause of the fatherless and plead the widow's case." Isn't it interesting that again in the context of worship, God asks us to 'do right'. He said the same thing to Cain when he made that first offering, 'Do what is right.'

In effect, there is the implication that the expressions of worship that they were bringing, whilst they were ignoring the cause of the oppressed, the fatherless and the widow, were in some way, 'evil deeds'. This may be the most shocking thing some folks have heard in a long time – hey, see that beautiful song of worship you're playing, with the neat melody and fine words and apparently sincere expression – if that is all there is, it's nothing more than an evil deed!

It occurs to me that a simple logical conclusion can be made here. To encourage the oppressed, feed the hungry, plead for the widow, is unlikely to be seen in God's eyes as an evil deed. I can find no place in Scripture, either by implication or by example, where God is angry because someone has done or is doing these things. Interesting, eh? But there is more than one example where men bring a worship offering to God with all the appropriate style and technique required, and yet fall very short of their purpose, because of their heart attitude or lack of integrity.

I believe in our world today we have got this slightly back to front. Somehow or other we have elevated the activity of sung or played worship to a level where we are upset if the quality or style isn't up to a perceived standard and yet, with regard to our programs for the poor and disadvantaged of this world, we are quite content to make do with whatever we've got.

Reading Isaiah, it seems that God would gladly trade a well-presented song of praise for a heart of compassion for the poor.

The thing is, this doesn't mean that we set aside our musical or liturgical worship and fling ourselves solely into ministry to the poor. In doing so we would simply be making another decision based on form and style, rather than the heart. Serving the poor, per se, does not equal 'great worship'.

No. More simply, it is this.

If in the giving of our worship we are engaged by the risen Christ and our hearts are fully exercised in giving Him praise and worship, then in that moment of revelation, we will find such a burden for the oppressed and disadvantaged of this world, the Father's heart if you like, that we will be fully convicted of our need to express worship to the Father by giving to the poor.

Get it? Jesus' revelation always results in a reaction in the hearts of men.

That's the reality. You can't separate worship and blessing the poor, because once you connect in worship with the heart of the Father, you will begin to touch His passion for the poor.

This is why one of the most successful ministry endeavours in the USA and Canada is the Compassion ministry for child sponsorship combining with worship events all over the country.

Connect in all honesty in worship with God, and you will connect with His heartbeat for the poor.

Around 15 years ago I attended a midweek special meeting in my home church with an invited speaker. The subject, close to our heart at the time, was the work of God in Ireland, north and south, and the reconciliation of the cultures and divisions in that society.

The visiting speaker was attempting to explain the history of Ireland and the reasons why things were as they were in our society at that time. This is always a big mistake in a place like Belfast, as, if nothing else is certain, you can be sure that 100 people in a room will have 100 different opinions as to 'why things are the way they are!' And just because they're all lovely Christians doesn't mean they will simply sit quietly and take your opinions!

I knew the speaker was in trouble when during the talk a heckler rose from his seat and shouted the words, "Rubbish! You don't know what you're talking about!"

Shock, horror! Somebody heckled the preacher! Isn't church fun these days?

"Now, now," said our invited guest, "you'll never understand what God is doing in Ireland unless you understand this talk."

Well done them, I suppose, for having the presence of mind to respond so swiftly. Either that or it wasn't the first time it had happened!

But here was the thing. If what the speaker was saying was right, I was in real trouble, as, to be honest, I had lost the entire train of thought some time earlier in the evening as I listened. My brain had been entirely bamboozled by the whole talk.

I don't remember much of the rest of the evening apart from the drive home in my car. I was somewhat sad, and disheartened. I did want to be of some use in helping to reconcile the fragmented pieces of our broken community here in Northern Ireland; I did want to find justice and righteousness and address oppression in my community, but if the key to finding my role there was in understanding the talk I had heard that night – then I was stuffed! I hadn't understood one iota of it!

Did this mean I could be of no use to my community?

Well, I wrote a song that night on the way home.

Northern Ireland is a small place so I should point out that the ride back home was no more than around 5 or 10 minutes. But in those few minutes the following words were composed of a song that, although it seems odd for worship writers to say such a thing, is still my favourite self-penned song of all that I have written.

The words of one portion of the song are as follows:
When earthly wisdom dims the light of knowing You.
Or if my search for understanding clouds Your way.
To You I'll fly, my hiding place,
Where revelation is beholding face to face.
(© Daybreak Music, 1998)

It's the last phrase in particular. Beholding in worship the face of Christ brings revelation. All the way through the Gospels, people confronted with the honesty and veiled majesty of Jesus – from Nathaniel to Zacchaeus, from Matthew to the Centurion, from the rich young ruler to Pilate himself – knew exactly what they should do and what they should pursue. Beholding the face of God in worship should bring revelation to the soul for life.

That's why worship without any compulsion to serve or care or bless the poor and disadvantaged of this world is such an offence to God.

The other reference, or one of the many other references, we find for this assertion is in Amos 5:11-12, 21-24 ...

> You trample on the poor and force him to give you grain. Therefore, though you have built stone mansions, you will not live in them; though you have planted lush vineyards, you will not drink their wine. For I know how many are your offenses and how great your sins. You oppress the righteous and take bribes and you deprive the poor of justice in the courts. I hate, I despise your religious feasts; I cannot stand your assemblies. Even though you bring me burnt offerings and grain offerings, I will not accept them. Though you bring choice fellowship offerings, I will have no regard for them. Away with the noise of your songs! I will not listen to the music of your harps. But let justice roll on like a river, righteousness like a never-failing stream!

Once more, the issue of provision and protection of the poor and the provision of justice and righteousness in society are balanced against music and festival worship.

It's interesting to note that God even mentions the quality of the worship offering, describing the fellowship offerings as 'choice'. Even with these high quality offerings, because they are not undergirded and balanced by justice and righteousness to the poor and oppressed, are of no value and will not be accepted.

Remember the lesson that we learned from Cain when he brought his grain offering to God? It wasn't a matter of the quality of the offering, it was the heart behind it. And here, even though the offering be highly prized and exceptional just like the offering that Abel brought, if the heart behind the offering is wrong, then even that act of worship is nullified and worthless.

But I don't believe it's a 'chicken and egg' situation. Or even a pure cause and effect. That is to say, one action of worship follows another. The start of this chapter related the case of the worship leader turning away from the musical worship to minister to the poor. But my point would be that if that ministry to the poor was not fuelled and motivated by the revelation that comes from the place of worship before God's throne, then, inasmuch as it blesses the recipients, it may not be any more acceptable an act of worship than that brought by the self-absorbed and witless musician transported only by the quality of his playing ability.

No, the two go hand in hand and are equal. I come before the Lord in worship, with my whole heart, and as His heart is revealed then I am encouraged and motivated to live righteously and act graciously as an extension of that worship. And in the act of helping the poor and oppressed, I realise that though I do this to the least of my brethren, I actually am serving God Himself and my heart has more cause to sing praises to my King.

What if worship invaded everything we do?

We would be worship disciples, we would be praising soldiers, we would be WARRIOR POETS.

CHAPTER 17

The Lover's Heart

What was your first act of worship?

From your first cry at birth until now, can you recall an event or a situation that could be reasonably understood as the very first act of worship that you performed?

Here are a few suggestions which may have been some sort of initial expression of worship …

At some point in our childhood we recognised and clung to our mother, or to whoever it was that made the first bond with our tiny selves. At that time our entire sense of worth, security and wellbeing was bound up in being close to, or within earshot of, this person!

We worshipped them.

Perhaps in our formative years we became besotted with a celebrity, a sportsperson, a teacher, or whoever. They so inspired and engaged us that they became an object of private devotion in our lives. Can you recall staring lovingly at a poster on your bedroom wall for a few hours, transfixed and transported by the beauty of the one pictured there? You were engaging in an act of worship.

At some other point in our childhood we perhaps marvelled at some aspect of God's creation, like a flower, or a snowfall, or a kitten. We were enthralled by this new thing and wondered at its incredible beauty and existence.

Perhaps a little later on, in the midst of some great trial or small trouble, for the first time you prayed to the God that you naturally sensed was there, even if no one had told you about Him.

Later still, maybe it was the first time you released some of your finances into some aspect of His work.

Maybe it was the time you surrendered your life to Jesus.

These are but a few, random examples. And I would imagine that you would find some similar experience or action which would represent the first act of worship in your own life. That worship may have been directed to, as the Bible puts it, "the created rather than the creator" (Romans 1:25), but, whilst misdirected, it doesn't diminish the passion or truthfulness of the act. For the most part, it wouldn't have involved singing or making music. It was an act of the heart and an act formed deep down in our very being.

We were created to worship. We are commanded to worship in Exodus 20. We are called to worship by Jesus in Luke 10:27-28. We are implored to be worshippers by Paul in Romans 12:1-2.

We are beings whose natural inclination is to worship. It is what or who we worship that causes problems.

Within the modern Church, perhaps some of us have narrowed our definition of worship to one aspect of the practice of worship. Maybe we have conditioned ourselves to believe the worship time is a collection of songs during the corporate church service. We might have a broader view and believe that the entire service on a Sunday morning is our worship and that other expressions of creativity like meditation, literature, poetry and art are acts of worship also. Perhaps some of us have an understanding that the giving of our tithes and offerings constitutes an act of worship. Some others, echoing the Apostle Paul's request that we "present our bodies as a living sacrifice" (Romans 12:1-2), know that it has something to do with the way we live our daily lives.

But, and this is important, whatever our understanding of our worship expression, the practice, the form, the 'how we worship', appears to be of minimal importance when offset against the heart of our worship.

At least in God's opinion.

No matter how free our structure is, how radical our methodology, how traditional our practice, or how liturgical our presentation, it matters little if the lover's heart of our worship is not present. Some commentators will applaud this statement and tell us that the way we live our lives, our care for justice, integrity, right living and evangelism all correspond to true worship. But even this isn't the master key or the entire story. In fact, no matter how we live our lives, if our heart is not right, it will not do. To quote the Apostle Paul, "If I gave everything I have to the poor, and give up my body to be burned, but have not love, I am nothing" (1 Corinthians 13:3).

Indeed, we know that the converse is true. No matter how foolish and simple our actions, if it flows on the fulness, truthfulness, sacrifice and passion of the worshipping heart, it will surely exceed the most complex and well-crafted praise symphony that man could ever create. It may even exceed the greatest sacrificial giving that man could make in life.

It has everything to do with your heart, and little to do with your practice!

Again, as Amos the prophet says:

"I hate all your show and pretence – the hypocrisy of your religious festivals and solemn assemblies. I will not accept your burnt offerings and grain offerings. I won't even notice all your choice peace offerings. Away with your hymns of praise! They are only noise to my ears. I will not listen to your music, no matter how lovely it is. Instead, I want to see a mighty flood of justice, a river of righteous living that will never run dry."

And so we finish.

Right worship can have an incredible impact, in lives, in communities, in cities and in nations. Even in these times when we in the Church are arguing over styles and form and irrelevant matters like that, entire nations are heading for destruction because of misplaced worship. If only we could redirect them to the One who owns that worship, who deserves that worship, and who actually created us for that purpose, then might we not see those nations radically changed?

Of course, we would! Jesus, worshipped and glorified, changes everything.

I hope what has been unfolded here has been helpful. I trust some of it is memorable. I really hope that many of you have been inspired to see yourselves as the WARRIOR POETS of this generation and to understand that God consistently chooses the foolish things of this world to confuse, to defeat and overthrow the wise and those that think themselves wise.

I hope you will pursue the purposes for which God has called you and for which Jesus laid down His life.

I hope, I suppose, that when you think about putting on the whole armour of God and wonder what sort of soldier you may be in His army, at least a few of you might declare, "I am a WARRIOR POET of the 21st Century!"

BIBLIOGRAPHY

Texts and Books used in the preparation of, and as inspiration or motivation for, this book:

Carson, D A (Ed). *Worship by the Book*. Zondervan, 2002.

Gibbs, A P. *Worship, The Christian's Highest Occupation*. Walterick Publishers, 1950.

McManus, Erwin. *Uprising*. Nelson Books, 2004.

Morgenthaller, Sally. *Worship Evangelism*. Zondervan, 1995.

Nick Page. *And Now, Let's Move into a Time of Nonsense*. Authentic Media, 2004.

Peterson, David. *Engaging with God*. Intervarsity Press, 1992.

Tozer, A W. *Whatever Happened to Worship?*. Christian Publications, 1985.

Ward, Peter. *Selling Worship*. Paternoster Press, 2005.